# SOCIAL CONTROL AND THE PROLIFERATION OF JUVENILE COURT SERVICES

## THOMAS G. BLOMBERG

San Francisco, California
1978

Published By

R&E Research Associates, Inc.
4843 Mission Street
San Francisco, California 94112




Publishers
Robert D. Reed and Adam S. Eterovich

Library of Congress Card Catalog Number
77-90354


I.S.B.N.
0-88247-504-5

# CONTENTS

Page

Preface . . . . . . . . . . . . . . . . . . . . . . . . . .   ix

List of Charts . . . . . . . . . . . . . . . . . . . . . .   v

List of Tables . . . . . . . . . . . . . . . . . . . . . .   vii

CHAPTER 1:  JUVENILE COURT ORGANIZATION AND DECISION-MAKING   1

    Conceptual Framework . . . . . . . . . . . . . . . . .   4
    Organization Relations and Exchange . . . . . . . . .   6
    Study Overview . . . . . . . . . . . . . . . . . . . .   10

CHAPTER 2:  HISTORICAL BACKGROUND OF CALIFORNIA JUVENILE
            COURT SERVICES . . . . . . . . . . . . . . . .   15

    Rise of the Child Saving Movement . . . . . . . . . .   15
    Establishment of Juvenile Courts . . . . . . . . . . .   16
    Search for Uniformity in Juvenile Court Services . .    20
    Ambiguity of County Juvenile Court Practices . . . .    25
    Early County Juvenile Court and Probation Experience    26

CHAPTER 3:  BOYS' TREATMENT CENTER:  A LOCAL INSTITUTION
            ALTERNATIVE TO STATE REFORMATORIES. . . . . .    31

    History of California's Camp, Ranch, and School
        Subsidy Acts . . . . . . . . . . . . . . . . . . .   34
    Role of Local Groups in Boys' Treatment Center
        Development . . . . . . . . . . . . . . . . . . .    38
    Boys' Center Operation . . . . . . . . . . . . . . . .   41
    Impact Assessment . . . . . . . . . . . . . . . . . .    43

CHAPTER 4:  PROBATION SUBSIDY:  AN INTENSIVE HOME
            SUPERVISION ALTERNATIVE TO STATE
            REFORMATORIES . . . . . . . . . . . . . . . .    52

    Growth Crisis in the State Youth Authority's
        Correctional System . . . . . . . . . . . . . . .    52
    Solution to the State's Correctional Explosion:
        Local Intensive Home Supervision . . . . . . . . .   54
    Probation Subsidy and the State Quest for Local
        Compliance . . . . . . . . . . . . . . . . . . . .   55
    Probation Subsidy Legislation . . . . . . . . . . . .    58
    Local Perception of Probation Subsidy . . . . . . . .    60
    Operation of Intensive Home Supervision Units . . .     63
    Probation Subsidy Impact . . . . . . . . . . . . . .     66

CHAPTER 5:   DIVERSION:  A FAMILY TREATMENT ALTERNATIVE TO
             JUVENILE COURT PROCESSING . . . . . . . . . . .      72

      Diversion:  A Federal Trend  . . . . . . . . . .      73
      California's Development of Diversion into Youth
        Service Bureaus  . . . . . . . . . . . . . . .      77
      Local Adaptation to the Diversion Trend  . . . . .    79
      Diversion Program Operation  . . . . . . . . . . .    81
      Diversion Program Impact . . . . . . . . . . . . .    87

CHAPTER 6:   ACCELERATED SOCIAL CONTROL AND THE FUTURE OF
             JUVENILE JUSTICE . . . . . . . . . . . . . . .      93

BIBLIOGRAPHY . . . . . . . . . . . . . . . . . . . . . .       98

APPENDIX . . . . . . . . . . . . . . . . . . . . . . . .      108

LIST OF CHARTS

Chart 1    Selected Exchange Relations in a County Juvenile
           Court System . . . . . . . . . . . . . . . . . .    8

Chart 2    State Probation Subsidy-Special Supervision  . . .   62

Chart 3    State Reformatory Commitments  . . . . . . . . . .   64

Chart 4    Diversion Program Components . . . . . . . . . . .   81

LIST OF TABLES

Table 1    Yearly Juvenile Hall Admi-sions, Daily Average
           Population and Yearly State Reformatory Commit-
           ments . . . . . . . . . . . . . . . . . . . . . . .    34

Table 2    Yearly Juvenile Hall Admissions, Daily Average
           Population and Yearly State Reformatory Commit-
           ments . . . . . . . . . . . . . . . . . . . . . . .    34

Table 3    The Development of County Treatment Institutions
           in California for Juveniles 1945-1970 . . . . . .     36

Table 4    County Youth Population, Arrests, Juvenile Court
           Intake Referrals of Delinquent Boys' Cases, and
           Subsequent Disposition of Intake Referrals  . . .     45

Table 5    Summary Totals of Delinquent Boys' Cases Under
           Some Form of Juvenile Court or State Reformatory
           Control . . . . . . . . . . . . . . . . . . . . . .   46

Table 6    Comparison of An Expected and An Estimated Number
           of Delinquent Boys Under State Reformatory Control
           in 1960-62 With Actual Number of Delinquent Boys
           Under State Reformatory Control . . . . . . . . . .   48

Table 7    Reasons for the Court Intake Referral of Delin-
           quent Boys' Cases Before Boys' Center 1957-59 . .     49

Table 8    Reasons for the Court Intake Referral of Delin-
           quent Boys' Cases After Boys' Center 1960-62  . .     49

Table 9    County Youth Population, Arrests, Juvenile Court
           Intake Referrals, and Subsequent Disposition of
           Intake Referrals . . . . . . . . . . . . . . . . .    67

Table 10   Summary Totals of Delinquent Cases Under Some
           Form of Juvenile Court or State Reformatory
           Control . . . . . . . . . . . . . . . . . . . . . .   68

Table 11   Comparison of An Expected and An Estimated Number
           of Delinquent Cases Under State Reformatory Con-
           trol in 1966-68 With Actual Number of Delinquent
           Cases Under State Reformatory Control . . . . . .     69

Table 12   County Youth Population, Arrests, Juvenile Court
           Intake Referrals, and Subsequent Disposition of
           Intake Referrals . . . . . . . . . . . . . . . . .    88

Table 13   Summary Totals of Youth Under Some Form of Ju-
           venile Court or Diversion Control as a Result of
           Direct Court Intake Referrals and Indirect Sibling
           Referrals to Diversion's Family Intervention . . .   88

Table 14   Comparison of the Expected Number of Youth Under
           Control in 1972 with Actual Number of Youth Under
           Control Including a Two Sibling Estimate  . . . .   90

# Preface

Since inception of the juvenile court, criticism has been focused on the lack of services available to accomplish the court's goals of individualized treatment and rehabilitation of troubled youths. It is commonly assumed that expansion of court services will result in more effective youth treatment and thereby reduce subsequent delinquent involvement. This study documents the movement of a California county juvenile court system from a limited youth supervision agency to a county level correctional establishment complete with diagnostic, institution, parole, and various community-based youth and family services. The development of these services is demonstrated to have been influenced heavily by conscious federal and state policies including significant funding assistance. Results of these services included accelerated court control of youths. Explanation and assessment of the study's implications focuse on the organization and decision-making characteristics of local juvenile court systems and the potential of accelerated control to reduce, create, or intensify delinquency.

In the course of developing this work, both during the original dissertation writing and later revisions, I have become indebted to a number of persons. I wish to thank Sheldon Messinger and Jerome Skolnick. I am especially indebted to Sheldon Messinger for criticism and encouragement. Additionally, I thank the personnel of the county juvenile court and probation department studied and the personnel of California Youth Authority's Division of Research and Development. Further, I would like to acknowledge my appreciation to Jeanine Blomberg, Sherry Caraballo, and Richard Delaplain, who assisted me in the organization of data and in editing.

Finally, for their perserverance and continued support I thank Jeanine and Tommy.

# CHAPTER 1

## JUVENILE COURT ORGANIZATION AND DECISION-MAKING

In 1967 a presidential report concluded that the country's juvenile courts had not been successful in rehabilitating problem youths or stemming the rising rates of youthful criminality. The report noted that courts had not accomplished their most basic function--bringing justice and compassion to youths in trouble. In addition, the court was found to have had a stigmatizing effect on youths it processed, thereby perpetuating the youths' delinquency. In light of these findings, the report recommended dealing with youths in trouble through means other than the formal juvenile justice system. The report argued:

> There should be expanded use of community agencies for dealing with delinquents nonjudicially and close to where they live. Use of community agencies has several advantages. It avoids the stigma of being processed by an official agency regarded by the public as an arm of crime control. It substitutes for official agencies organizations better suited for redirecting conduct.[1]

Criticism of delinquency control agencies represents a departure from the major focus of previous research on youthful deviance. Most studies have emphasized the importance of individual, group, or environmental causes of youthful crime in determining means of delinquency prevention and control.

Recent studies have broadened the area of delinquency inquiry to include the role of such institutions as the schools, police, and juvenile courts in the delinquency control process. The "societal reaction" or "labeling" school views delinquency in relation to these agencies. The two primary assumptions of this school are that (1) agencies of social control categorize youth according to such criteria as race, dress, and demeanor and then focus attention on them and (2) through this process these agencies create or at least support delinquency.[2]

Empirical studies reflecting the labeling approach include a study of police encounters with juveniles by Briar and Piliavin, a report on selection of young offenders for court by Goldman, and an inquiry into the relationship between gang members and the police by Piliavin and Werthman.[3] Aaron Cicourel, in a four year study of police, probation, and juvenile court, also focuses on issues in the delinquent labeling process. This study emphasizes the role of everyday activities, judgments, and practical decision-making by youths and juvenile justice agency personnel. In evaluating his approach, Cicourel contends:

> A question like "What 'forces' motivate or struc-
> ture the entrance into delinquent activity?" misses
> the general relevance of the problem of practical rea-
> soning that juveniles engage in when pursuing daily
> activities, how the police and probation officials
> are drawn into contact with juveniles, and how the
> police or probation officers decide that particular
> events fall under general policies or rules deemed
> relevant.[4]

Cicourel maintains that the empirical study of juvenile justice
agencies raises basic issues about how juveniles are labeled delinquent.

Moreover, Cicourel's work can be described as an attempt to
discover the nature of socially organized activities.  He provides
a significant methodological contribution in this regard.  He contends that language has a specific bearing on case outcome and
that the juvenile justice system cannot be understood without
recognition of the unreported aspects of cases.  He writes:

> . . . conversational procedures that occur in natural
> settings in everyday life are not only a rich source
> of information about how members communicate with
> (understand) each other, how the researcher can gain
> insight into member's practical reasoning or decision-
> making, how members communicate the significance of
> rules, social identities, and the like, but also pro-
> vides the basis for understanding something about
> how history is created.[5]

Blumberg and Emerson have combined labeling interest with organization inquiry in individual attempts to investigate the nature
of criminal and juvenile courts.  In discussing theoretical framework, Blumberg notes:

> We know the legal aspects of the process, but
> how shall we describe the social organization of the
> institutional mechanism which fastens the label
> 'criminal' on the individual?  We may be surprised
> to learn that formal legal structures, procedures
> and rules are not ultimately significant in discern-
> ing the nature of the criminal court.  Instead, the
> complex of organizational variables which defines
> the criminal court's social system and its interre-
> lated occupational and bureaucratic networks is the
> key to its apprehension.[6]

Emerson studied a metropolitan juvenile court to discover
how juvenile court response to problem youth is influenced by the
court's external context and internal dynamics.  This work inves-
tigates how the court defines, categorizes, and processes cases
in connection with the court's relationship with other agencies

in its institutional environment. The juvenile court is found to be a routinized institution that adapts to its organizational environment and in the adaptation process subverts its treatment goals. Emerson concludes:

> . . . in the course of negotiating with other agencies the juvenile court's treatment goals are subtly displaced. Treatment, as the court visualizes it, is compromised through the coercive and dumping uses made of its power. But even more significantly, treatment is undermined through court cooption into a system of placements biased against "delinquents." As a result, the court finds it cannot press too insistently for placement or treatment of "hardcore" cases as a condition for obtaining sympathetic consideration in milder and less threatening cases, despite its own conviction that the former have the same or even greater need for "help" in these terms.[7]

Thus, despite the previous tendency to dismiss the importance of social control agencies in delinquency research, a substantial interest and the beginning of empirical studies are emerging. The conclusions and recommendations drawn by the President's Task Force on Juvenile Delinquency and Youth Crime further demonstrates discontent with current juvenile justice practices and a substantial push for alternate strategies in dealing with problem youths.

The study on which this book is based seeks to add to current interest in the organization, operation, and impact of social control agencies by examining a California county's development of juvenile court treatment services. Treatment services are described in terms of their origin, operation, and subsequent impact on processing youths in the county juvenile court system.[8] This study's orientation can be contrasted to that of Cicourel and Emerson by its focus on juvenile court service development or organization context in explaining official response to problem youths. While acknowledging the importance of the organization context, Cicourel and Emerson emphasize specific ways juvenile court personnel deal with their caseloads. Their studies primarily attempt to describe decision-making patterns by juvenile court personnel in terms of the labeling approach.

This study focuses on both the development and subsequent decision-making consequences of a particular organization context. The idea here is that juvenile court decision-making or youth labeling patterns are not timeless, but are affected by the organization arrangements in which they take place and to which they have relevance. Further, these organization arrangements change over time because they are influenced by yet broader structural, economic, and cultural developments. This study is basically concerned with the connection between court decision-making or youth labeling patterns and court organization structure.

3

## Conceptual Framework

A major theoretical view underlying this study is that of the institutional school of organization inquiry.[9] This approach is unique in its view of an organization as a "whole." Specific processes, such as individual or small group activity and leadership, combine to form the whole of the organization and give the organization an identifiable character. The emphasis on organizations as wholes implies differences between organizations. Thus, research using this approach has tended to case studies with limited comparative findings. The case study approach usually analyzes the organization's past to explain how its present character has been shaped.[10] In reviewing the developmental emphasis of this approach, Perrow suggests:

> Because the interchange of structure and function goes on over time, a "natural history" of an organization is needed. We cannot understand current crises or competencies without seeing how they were shaped. The present is rooted in the past; no organization (and no man) is free to act as if the situation were de novo and the world a set of discret opportunities ready to be seized upon at will.[11]

Therefore, the questions that guide this approach revolve around an organization's attempts to reach satisfactory accommodations with its environment. These accommodations can lead to changes in the organization's goals or character.

Sheldon Messinger, Joseph Gusfield, Burton Clark, Philippe Nonet, David Sudnow, and others have written about a variety of organizations that have changed their goals in favor of the organization's growth or survival.[12] Sudnow, for example, focused on how a particular court handled its criminal cases. His findings indicated the public defender typically persuaded the defendent to plead guilty to a lesser charge following an agreement on the defendant's classification by the public defender and prosecutor. Sudnow found this negotiated classification and subsequent guilty plea on a lesser charge were not directly related to the facts of the case. In describing the public defender's activities with the defendant, Sudnow states:

> From the outset, the P.D. attends to establishing the typical character of the case before him and thereby instituting routinely employed reduction arrangements. The defendant's appearance - his race, demeanor, age, style of talk, way of attending to the occasion of his incarceration - provides the P.D. with the initial sense of his place in the social structure. Knowing only that the defendant is charged with section 459 (Burglary) of the penal code, the P.D. employs his conception of typical burglars against which the character of the present defendant is assessed.[13]

Defendants who refused the reduced charge in return for a guilty plea were placed in a different category. Special prosecutors strongly pursued their cases as punishment for their lack of cooperation. These classifications and routine responses allowed the court to handle its caseload efficiently but substantially detracted from the court's goals of due process. Several writers have provided similar analyses in the area of corrections.[14]

Perrow, who also used this approach, provides an interesting review of the institution approach. He contends the school's main contributions lie in three areas.

First, emphasis on the organization as a whole supports the conception that there is a variety of organizations. However, this variety is not so extensive that organizations cannot be classified for certain purposes according to basic organization characteristics. In terms of organization autonomy, for example, some organizations are extremely dependent on a variety of groups, agencies, etc., while others have considerable autonomy. Perrow points out:

> Large business and industrial organizations are largely autonomous, and for that reason leadership processes are presumably different, technology has more leeway, and bureaucratization is essential for efficiency. Prisons, mental hospitals, and many small welfare agencies exist to show that something is being done about some problems, but few care just what it is or how effective it is; those who control the organization's resources (legislators, religious boards, etc.) care only that the "something" should not involve scandals and should not cost too much. Here again, the environment for leadership, technology, and structure will be different, and inventories, elegant formal theories, and so on may miss the point.[15]

The second contribution that Perrow outlines is the possibility that organizations take on a life of their own independent of their formal purposes or the wishes of those in control. Selznick's distinction[16] between organization and institution is an attempt to conceptualize this process. The difference is between the rational, mechanical, and "no nonsense" systems view of organizations versus the responsive, adaptive, natural-life-of-its-own concept applied to an institution.[17] While neither of these positions adequately describes the workings and character of most organizations, the organization-institution distinction has important implications for the understanding of organizations. For example, a number of predictive implications of the organization model may be used in viewing a county juvenile court as a rational tool devised mechanically to dispense technical services to a particular clientele. The rational model might lead to the prediction that the juvenile court organization will quickly respond to its environment even to the point of termination if its role is no longer purposeful in terms of its client-service goal. In contrast, the institution model would lead to prediction that the juvenile court organization would attempt to influence its environment to fulfill its own organization needs. The life-of-its-own concept views the organization as responsive to varieties of pressures and opportunities that are not necessarily related to client "needs" as in the rational model but that reflect concern with survival, maintenance, or expansion of the organization. This rational-adaptive distinction raises the important question of who is served by the organization.[18]

Third, the environment emphasis provides the dominant contribution of the institution school. Detailed analysis of the interaction between the organization and its environment provides the organization's story. Through this process of interaction the organization grows, declines, or changes. Organizations must continually adapt or improvise to keep in favor with their chief sources of support. The organization's environment provides its resources. The more successful the organization is in maintaining its environmental relationships, the greater its likelihood for fulfilling its needs for maintenance and growth.

However, according to Perrow, the institutional school is most lacking in this environmental area. There has not been a systematic connection between the environment and the organization.

> Parts of the "environment" are seen as affecting
> organizations, but the organization is not seen as
> defining, creating, and shaping its environment.
> We live in an "organizational society" the insti-
> tutionalists routinely announce, but the significant
> environment of organizations is not "society;" they
> do not realize that it is other organizations, and
> generally other organizations that share the same
> interest, definitions of reality and power.[19]

Therefore, it is overly simplistic to describe an organization's role within its environment as essentially adaptive. By necessity organizations are concerned with their needs and seek environment support in accordance with these perceived needs. Unfortunately, an organization's quest for support through environment interaction has been both underestimated and understudied in organization research. One reason for this has been the failure to describe what constitutes the environment of various organizations. Perrow's suggestion concerning the "significant environment" of organizations being other organizations with similar interests provides helpful assistance in this regard.[20]

## Organization Relations and Exchange

Several recent works have begun to examine organization relations in terms of exchange activity. This involves viewing organization networks as systems of interdependent interests. According to Gore, formal organizations are embedded "in an environment of other organizations as well as in a complex of norms, values, and collectivities of the society."[21] Organizations and their environmental constituents are interdependent components of a larger system. They reflect their interdependency through exchange relationships. Exchange between organizations need not involve direct reciprocal activity, but can include activity directed toward realization of each organization's goals. In the juvenile justice system a number of exchange relations between agencies are necessary to meet the formal and informal needs and goals of the various interrelated agencies. Beyond officially connected agencies (such as the police, juvenile court, and corrections) other interconnected groups are involved in the exchange process. For instance, the county juvenile court organization under study had developed ongoing exchange relations with a range of groups including the county's Superior Court Judges Committee, the Grand Jury, the Juvenile Justice Commission, the League of Women Voters, Lawyers' Wives, Women's Auxiliary, and other citizen groups. The interaction between the court organization and these groups varies in frequency and the nature of exchange is not always obvious. Describing variety of exchange relations, Cole writes:

> Although mere interaction does not of necessity mean that exchange will occur, these social contacts lead to the development of relations in which the aim of each participant is to safeguard his own interest. Through the recognition of these interests exchanges may be developed which will benefit both partners.[22]

In this relationship, the safeguard of interests, "domain consensus" is required. When organizations interact and their functions are not obvious, consensus must be negotiated. Attempt to achieve at least minimal consensus is the reason for most organization interaction. Levine and White contend:

> These processes of achieving domain consensus constitute much of the interaction between organizations. While they may not involve the immediate flow of elements, they are often necessary preconditions for the exchange of elements, because without at least minimal domain consensus there can be no exchange among organizations.[23]

The effort to establish domain consensus is well demonstrated in the California juvenile justice system, especially in state and county roles. While statutes attempt to establish consensus they fall short. Patterns of competition, negotiation, and cooperation result between agencies over jurisdiction, functions, the receipt of resources, etc. For example, to clarify the relationship between county court services and the California Youth Authority ongoing negotiations have been conducted concerning varieties of issues that the formal statutes fail to delineate.[24] The differences between the functions of county juvenile court systems and the Youth Authority are not at all clear. The Youth Authority, as it turns out, has far greater access to financial resources.

Over the years the Youth Authority has been able to secure a degree of consensus through administration of financial subsidies and technical services to counties. State subsidies entail the dispensing of money to local jurisdictions in return for local implementation of specific functions directed toward achieving state goals. This exchange has facilitated a working relationship between the two jurisdictions with a reasonable level of specialization and helped limit duplication of services. However, the negotiable character of this division of functions must be emphasized to understand the nature of these relationships and their implications.

Similar exchange relationships take place between the county court organization and other local groups that comprise its significant environment, as well as the California Council on Criminal Justice, a state administrative agency that distributes federal funds. Several selected exchange relations with the county juvenile court system under study are displayed in Chart 1. The structural context and the types of resources that flow between the court system and these organizations varies and requires specification. By definition, exchange between two organizations involves activity that has either actual or anticipated consequences "for the realization of their respective goals or objectives."[25]

CHART 1

SELECTED EXCHANGE RELATIONS IN A
COUNTY JUVENILE COURT SYSTEM

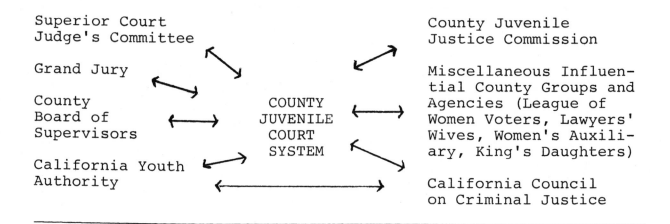

Exchange can take the form of either (1) cooperation or (2) bargaining. Cole points out that the difference between these forms hinges on the question: "Were the conditions for the transfer of resources negotiated?"[26]

In terms of cooperative exchange each organization recognizes that it is in its interest to be involved in the transfer of resources with another organization without negotiation.  It is understood that cooperation is productive for both parties. This type of exchange activity is reflected in the normal working relations of police and juvenile court in the routine processing of youths.

Exchange relations characterized by bargaining involve the negotiation of conditions before the exchange of resources between two organizations.  This process occurs when persons from each organization set the conditions under which the exchange will be based.  In this instance, the juvenile court's probation officer could meet with representatives of the county's Juvenile Justice Commission to discuss a needed expansion in court services.[27] The probation officer would attempt to persuade commission representatives of the appropriateness of the expansion in question to gain their support and subsequent political influence with the County Board of Supervisors for funding allocations.  The Commission representatives, on the other hand, want to support changes that will reflect well on their own organizations and ease their operating problems.  Thus, for exchange to occur there must be negotiations about the change and its implications that lead to some level of consensus between the two organizations.  Cole points out that bargaining of this nature "involves a strategy of compromise:  a system of incentives by which all parties are brought to agree to the (final) settlement."[28]

Bargaining for the exchange of resources between organizations is continual despite fairly dependable environment resources. However, the importance of exchange is especially dramatic when organization expansion is involved.  Thompson and McEwen write:

> Even where fairly stable and dependable expecta-
> tions have been built up with important elements of the
> organizational environment - with suppliers, distribu-
> tors, legislators, workers and so on - the organiza-
> tion cannot assume that these relationships will con-
> tinue.  Periodic review of these relationships must
> be accomplished, and an important means for this is
> bargaining, whereby each organization, through nego-
> tiation, arrives at a decision about future behavior
> satisfactory to the others involved.[29]

In the adjustment of relationships, organizations attempt to control their significant environment--those organizations, groups, or individuals that have influence over their operation.  Environment control can take a variety of forms each of which is aimed at initiating, maintaining, or strengthening environment relations for eventual exchange.  The extent of an organization's success in bargaining substantially determines its access to resources.  Resources available to an organization also may determine its success at bargaining.  Access to resources provides the organization effective means for realizing various goals.  Therefore, from this perspective it can be concluded that organization goals, functions, and accomplishments are very much a product of ongoing political negotiations, compromises, and exchanges between organizations.

## Study Overview

The purpose of the study is to investigate the consequences resulting from the adaptable nature of a California county juvenile court system. This adaptable organization character is viewed as a result of vague legislation, unclear goals, technology, and financial instability that characterize local juvenile court systems. These adaptive characteristics are seen as facilitating varieties of organization developments that, in turn, structure the court's capacity to "discover" and deal with different categories of youthful problems. Stated differently, the determination of "delinquent in need of court service" is, in part, determined by organization context. The organization's context provides a framework of constraining client definitions and corresponding court service alternatives that change over time in relation to the organization's response to various pressures and opportunities. Organization definitions in a county juvenile court system are directly related to such disposition alternatives as formal home supervision, foster homes, institution treatment facilities, psychiatric counseling services, and other program alternatives. These organization alternatives provide the structural determinants of juvenile court related decision-making. They comprise the system of action in which the juvenile court judge and probation personnel must operate, thereby, significantly affecting their range of official decisions pertaining to troubled youths. Therefore, it can be argued that decision-making by juvenile justice personnel is a product of a particular organization context that fluctuates over time and across jurisdictions.

Proceeding from this organization model of decision-making, this study will focus on three court service developments: boys' treatment center, a county residential treatment alternative to state reformatories; probation subsidy, an intensive home supervision alternative to state reformatories; and diversion, a whole family treatment alternative to formal juvenile court handling. Each of the three court service developments will be analyzed in terms of their origin and the specific organization procedures involved in their local implementation. Additionally, the operation and the impact of each development will be described and measured.

The following arguments will be developed in relation to the county's reasoning for the three court service developments and their subsequent decision-making impact. First, the county juvenile court system does not have consensus on its goals, practices, and clientele. Second, the three investigated court services-- boys' treatment center, probation subsidy, and diversion--have been developed in connection with perceived organization needs instead of in response to explicit client needs. Third, these organization expansions are the result of opportunity, interaction, and exchange between the county court system and other local, state, and federal organizations. Fourth, the operation and decision-making consequences of these expansions have been to provide a sizeable increase in the court's capacity to deal with youths and, in the case of diversion, their families. Fifth, the increase in the court's youth and family control capacity was influenced greatly by consciously designed state and federal policies and centralized funding. Local authonomy has been reduced because of the local jurisdiction's dependence on centralized funds while coordination between local, state, and federal levels has increased. In this environment, a substantially expanded correctional network and control capacity has evolved.

A underlying assumption in this study is that new court service programs result in a "program magnet phenomenon."[30] New programs must have a clientele. Therefore, a proportion of clients formerly suitable for an existing program are displaced into a new program. Often, however, program client displacement is not sufficient, so new clients previously not considered in need of service are judged suitable for service within a less constrained service alternative structure.

The arguments that guide this study correspond with the institutional model of organizations, which emphasizes adaptiveness. This organizational orientation corresponds to what Packer has described as the crime-control model of justice.[31] Packer contrasts this crime-control model with the due-process model. The due-process model parallels the rational, consciously-planned conception of organizations. In adapting Packer's design to juvenile justice, two models emerge analogous to those Packer presents for the adult justice system. The client-centered model emphasizes non-adversary and individualized treatment goals. It views juvenile justice as a process whereby troubled youths are individually diagnosed and treated without legal consideration or complications. The organization-dominance model de-emphasizes individualized treatment and the non-adversary nature of the juvenile justice process. In this model, classification and processing of youths are directly related to available organization alternatives.[32]

To summarize, the juvenile court will be viewed as a formal organization that operates with conflicting goals, limited technology, and financial variability. These characteristics produce operation uncertainty and facilitate an opportunistic response by the court to externally funded court service innovations which, in turn, structure the court's response to problem youths. As a result, the pattern of youth control administered by the court is significantly shaped by the organization alternatives available to the court. These organization alternatives vary over time and across court jurisdictions in response to the court's reaction to various state and federally funded court service innovations.

Finally, it should be noted that the present study makes no attempt to propose a new or more effective county juvenile court system. Rather, its goal is to provide an empirical contribution to the literature concerning juvenile court organization and decision-making.

FOOTNOTES--CHAPTER 1

<sup></sup>¹The President's Commission on Law Enforcement and Adminis-
tration of Justice. Task Force Report:  Juvenile Delinquency and
Youth Crime (1967), p. 19.

²For an analysis of recent delinquency research and labeling theory see Richard H. Ward, "The Labeling Theory:  A Critical
Analysis," Criminology An Inter-disciplinary Journal, 9 (1971),
p. 268.

³See S. Briar and I. Piliavin, "Police Encounters With Juveniles," in R. Giallombardo (ed.), Juvenile Delinquency:  A Book
of Readings (1966); N. Goldman, The Differential Selection of Juvenile Offenders for Court Appearance (1963); I. Piliavin and C.
Werthman, "Gang Members and the Police," in D. Bordua (ed.), The
Police (1967).

⁴Aaron Cicourel, The Social Organization of Juvenile Justice
(1968), pp. 168-169.

⁵Cicourel, The Social Organization of Juvenile Justice, p.
167.

⁶Abraham S. Blumberg, Criminal Justice (1967), p. ix.

⁷Robert M. Emerson, Judging Delinquents Context and Process
in Juvenile Court (1969), p. 80.

⁸The term "county juvenile court system" refers to both the
juvenile court and the probation department which serves the
court.

⁹The institutional school is best represented in the writ-
ings of Philip Selznick.  See his "Foundations of a Theory of Organization," American Sociological Review, 13 (1948), p. 25;
TVA and the Grass Roots (1965); and Leadership in Administration
(1957).

¹⁰For a review of the methodological approach employed in
the current study see Appendix.

¹¹Charles Perrow, Complex Organizations:  A Critical Essay
(1972), p. 178.

¹²Sheldon L. Messinger, "Organizational Transformation:  A
Case Study of Declining Social Movement," American Sociological
Review, 20 (1955), p. 3; Joseph Gusfield, Symbolic Crusade:  Sta-
tus Politics and the American Temperance Movement (1963); Burton
Clark, The Open Door College:  A Case Study (1960); Philippe
Nonet, Administrative Justice:  Advocacy and Change in Government
Agencies (1969); David Sudnow, "The Public Defender," in R.
Schwartz and J. Skolnick (eds.), Society and the Legal Order
(1970).

[13]Sudnow, "The Public Defender", p. 392.

[14]For example, see Donald R. Cressey, "Achievement of an Un-
stated Organizational Goal: An Observation on Prisons," Pacific
Sociological Review, 1 (1958), p. 43; and Gresham M. Sykes, The
Society of Captives: A Study of a Maximum Security Prison (1958).
For reform schools, see Mayer N. Zald, "The Correctional Institu-
tion for Juvenile Offenders: An Analysis of Organizational
'Character'," Social Problems 8, No. 1 (Summer 1960), p. 57; and
David Street, Robert Vinter and Charles Perrow, Organizations for
Treatment (1966).

[15]Perrow, Complex Organizations: A Critical Essay, pp. 187-
188.

[16]Selznick, Leadership in Administration, pp. 5-22.

[17]For a critical elaboration of the organizational-institu-
tional distinction see Sheldon S. Wolin, "A Critique of Organizational Theories," in Amitai Etzioni (ed.), A Sociological Reader
on Complex Organizations, 2nd ed. (1969), pp. 133-149.

[18]Perrow, Complex Organizations: A Critical Essay, pp. 188-
189.

[19]Perrow, Complex Organizations: A Critical Essay, p. 199.

[20]Perrow, Complex Organizations: A Critical Essay, pp. 199-
204.

[21]William J. Gore, Administrative Decision-Making: A
Heuristic Model (1964), p. 22.

[22]George E. Cole, Politics and the Administration of Justice
(1973), p. 58.

[23]Sol Levine and Paul E. White, "Exchange as a Conceptual
Framework for the Study of Interorganizational Relationships,"
in Amitai Etzioni (ed.), A Sociological Reader on Complex Organizations, (1969) p. 131.

[24]The California Youth Authority administers the state youth
reformatories and parole services which the county juvenile courts
use for placement of their most serious youth cases.

[25]S. Levine and P. White, "Exchange as a Conceptual Framework for the Study of Interorganizational Relationships," in
Amitai Etzioni (ed.), A Sociological Reader on Complex Organizations, p. 121.

[26]Cole, Politics and the Administration of Justice, p. 62.

[27]The Juvenile Justice Commission is an eight member citizen
board that is formally responsible for the supervision and yearly
written assessment of county juvenile probation services. See

[28]Cole, Politics and the Administration of Justice, p. 63.

[29]James D. Thompson and William J. McEwen, "Organizational Goals and Environment," in Amitai Etzioni (ed.), A Sociological Reader on Complex Organizations, 2nd ed. (1969), p. 193.

[30]See California Youth and Adult Corrections Agency, Report, 1967, pp. 89-90.

[31]See Herbert L. Packer, "Two Models of the Criminal Process," University of Pennsylvania Law Review, 113 (1964), p. 1.

[32]For further discussion on Packer's contrasting models of criminal justice and corresponding organizational models see Cole, Politics and the Administration of Justice, pp. 53-56.

CHAPTER 2


HISTORICAL BACKGROUND OF CALIFORNIA JUVENILE COURT SERVICES


     This study examines a county's development of juvenile court
services over a fifteen year period.  A selective approach to historical materials has been taken.  The areas considered in this
chapter are the rise of youth corrections in the United States,
California's early juvenile court act and amendments, and the
state's administrative activities related to county juvenile court
practices.  The latter areas were included to describe legal and
administrative constraints, involved in county development of juvenile court services.  A review of the county's early experience
with juvenile court services will be provided as background to
the subsequent chapters.  This study shows how the early roots of
county juvenile courts relate to emergence of an ambiguous organizational enterprise.


Rise of the Child Saving Movement

     Institutionalization of deviant people began in the early
nineteenth century and coincided with the period's belief that society could not maintain social order without organized reform.
The basic premise was that crime did not reflect an inherent de-
pravity in man; but, rather, was the consequence of a fragmented
society.

     Belief in the perfectibility of man and this premise about
the causes of deviant behavior led to development of the correctional institution.  The underlying idea of correctional institutions was that an uncorrupt environment--emphasizing work, order,
routine, and discipline--would provide inmates the moral and phys-
ical abilities needed to combat the inherent dangers of the society.  Rothman states:

          The promise of institutionalization depended upon
     the isolation of the prisoner and the establishment
     of a disciplined routine.  Convinced that deviancy
     was primarily the result of the corruptions pervad-
     ing the community, and that organizations like the
     family and the church were not counterbalancing them
     they believed that a setting which removed the offend-
     er from all temptations and substituted a steady and
     regular regimen would reform him.  Since the convict
     was not inherently depraved, but the victim of an
     upbringing that had failed to provide protection
     against the vices at loose in society, a well-ordered
     institution could successfully reeducate and rehabili-

15

tate him. The penitentiary, free of corruption and dedicated to the proper training of the inmate, would inculcate the discipline that negligent parents, evil companions, taverns, houses of prostitution, theaters, and gambling halls had destroyed. Just as the criminal's environment had led him into crime, the institutional environment would lead him out of it.[1]

The two central functions of the youth reformatory (or house of refuge, as it was referred to in the early nineteenth century) were to (1) provide shelter from an "improper" environment and (2) rehabilitate, reform, or change young deviants into law-abiding citizens. As in the mental hospital and penitentiary, the reformatory was to accomplish people-changing through a program emphasizing order, routine, discipline, and strict obedience. Platt states, "The reformatory system was based on the assumption that proper training can counteract the impositions of poor family life, a corrupt environment, and poverty, while at the same time toughening and preparing delinquents for the struggle ahead."[2] Correctional reformers assumed deviants were susceptible to change. Youth offenders, were thought to be especially pliable, since they were not as fixed on deviant life styles as were adult offenders.

Between 1825 and 1830 New York, Boston, and Philadelphia established houses of refuge. However, separate facilities for delinquent youths were slow to develop. Many urban centers used orphanages as multifunction institutions. But, between 1840 and 1857 specialization had increased and seventeen reformatories were operating with a combined inmate population of more than 20,000.[3]

The 1850's were a significant period in development of juvenile reformatories primarily because of growing disillusionment with the penitentiary. During this decade it became evident that prisons were not fulfilling their people-changing promise. Therefore, interest was renewed in differentiating between juvenile and adult offenders. This distinction was made because of the belief that youthful deviants were more susceptible to character change. At the close of the nineteenth century, juvenile courts became more prevalent across the United States, as a means to further differentiate processing of youthful offenders from that of adult offenders.

## Establishment of Juvenile Courts

California enacted a juvenile court law in 1903 after strong lobbying by several women's groups. These groups argued that children's cases were being heard with and in a manner similar to adult cases. This assertion is partially substantiated by state reform school commitments. For example, of the total number of boys committed to California's Preston School of Industry before 1900, 70 percent were committed by the superior court (i.e., the criminal court) and the remaining 30 percent by police, justices, and recorders' courts.[4]  However, many youthful offenders never reached the state reformatory level.  In many such instances treatment was provided through informal arrangements with the police, family, or local community.[5]

The issue of differential treatment before inception of the juvenile court is not of particular significance here.  However, it should be recognized that long before the juvenile courts youth were not, as a rule, incarcerated with adults; harsh sentences for trivial offenses were exceptions; and capital punishment for a juvenile offender was almost unknown.  Further, recent studies have suggested that saving children was not the only concern of persons who argued for founding the juvenile court.  The studies contend the "child savers" were interested in imposing middle-class white standards on urban youths of minority or immigrant backgrounds.  Therefore, in addition to criminal acts, juvenile court jurisdiction included such offenses as truancy, disobedience to parents, and "in danger of living an idle, lewd, or immoral life."[6]

Nonetheless, before advent of the juvenile court, youths involved in more serious offenses were being arrested and jailed. Of particular concern to the reformers, as Lemert points out, "was the visible aspects of juvenile justice--public arrests, transportation to jail in paddy wagons, open hearings in court along with criminals, misdemeanents, and prostitutes."[7]  These visible aspects provided the reformers with illustrations to emphasize their lobbying efforts.  Yet, despite impressive preparation, organization, and a statewide campaign, the 1903 California act was secured only after a compromise agreement that public funds would not be used for county probation officer salaries.

The 1903 act provided for state control, protection, and treatment of dependent as well as delinquent children.  This act applied to children under sixteen years.  Counties with more than one superior court judge were required to designate one judge or more to hear in special session cases coming under juvenile court jurisdiction.  There were three other major provisions of the 1903 act.[8]

1. No court could commit a child under 12 to a jail, prison, or police station; however, if such a child were unable to furnish bail, he could be committed to the care of the sheriff, police officer, constable, or probation officer.

2. The superior court of each county could appoint a board of six citizens to serve the county without compensation.  Their duties would be the investigation of all societies, associations, and corporations receiving children under this act.

3. Any judge of superior court should have the authority to appoint or designate one or more persons to act as probation officers and to serve at the pleasure of the court.

17

Because probation officer salaries could not be drawn from public funds, private sources were sought. In San Francisco County, for example, Boys and Girls' Aid Society, California Club, and Associated Charities provided probation officer salaries.[9]

In 1905 responding to recommendations by the Board of Charities and Corrections (predecessor to the State Department of Welfare), the legislature amended the 1903 act in several respects. The investigating board of six citizens was replaced by a seven member probation committee. Committee members were to be appointed by the county's superior court judges. Probation officers were to be appointed for two-year terms by the probation committees of each county and, significantly, their salaries were to come from the county.[20]

The next significant development in California's juvenile court movement occurred following the 1908 conference of the State Board of Charities and Corrections. The conference was attended by superior court judges, district attorneys, county probation committee members, and probation officers, as well as officials from the Whittier and Preston state reformatories. Purpose of the meeting was to discuss general problems with the existing juvenile court legislation and draw up recommendations to be presented to the state legislature. The following recommendations were adopted at the conference:[11]

1.  That the Probation Committee should be retained and that the power to nominate the probation officers is not unconstitutional and should be retained.

2.  That in the larger counties the law makes it mandatory upon the board of supervisors to provide a detention home.

3.  That probation officers should be paid a salary from the county treasury.

4.  That a parental or adult contributory delinquency and dependency law is necessary.

5.  That the age of majority for girls be raised from eighteen to twenty-one years.

6.  That the ages for commitment to both Whittier State School and Preston School of Industry be fixed at between nine and nineteen.

7.  That the laws governing the two reform schools be withdrawn so as to make them conform with respect to commitments, with the exception that girls be committed to Whittier only, and that the Preston School provide for the commitment of dependent male children.

8. That commitments to Whittier and Preston schools
   are to be considered rather in the nature of
   guardianship than as punishment for crimes, and
   these institutions as schools and not prisons.
   In such case, a trial by jury is not essential.

In 1909 the legislature responded with another juvenile
court law. This new legislation embodied most of the 1908 conference recommendations. Its major features were the following:

--Creation of a special court to deal with children.

--Requirement of a probation committee in each county.

--Placement of children on probation instead of in prison.

--Provision of a paid probation officer or officers for each
county.

--Severing of parents' rights to child custody in cases
where the welfare of the child requires it.

--Extension of juvenile court jurisdiction to adults found
to be contributing to the delinquency of a minor and making such
offense a misdemeanor.

A delinquent youth was defined in the 1909 legislation as
any person under eighteen years old who is found to have violated
any law of the state or any ordinance of a town, city, or county.

A dependent child was defined as a person under eighteen who
is found to be begging or receiving alms, in the streets or public
place for the purpose of begging, a vagrant, wandering without a
home or means of subsistence, without parent or guardian or without proper control, destitute, with an unfit home, in the company
of criminals or prostitutes, living or being in a house of prostitution, habitually frequenting places where liquors are sold, re-
fusing to obey reasonable parental orders or incorrigible, without
proper parents, habitually truant, or habitually using intoxicat-
ing liquors.[12]

In 1911 the juvenile court law was modified to include jurisdiction over all persons under the age of twenty-one. Probation officers were to be nominated by county probation committees
and appointed by the judges. However, by 1914 many judges and
probation officers felt the existing law was unworkable. That
year the Board of Charities and Corrections met and acknowledged
that there was general county dissatisfaction with the present
act. Lemert suggests that during this period there was conflict
between moral-reform groups and juvenile court officials.[13]
Judges and probation officers did not want to be restricted by
legal directives in handling children or removing them from parental custody. One Judge of this period commented:

I sincerely trust no attempt will be made to

prescribe the exact processes that the court should
follow in these cases. The legislature should lay
down the essentials which are to govern. That
ground has generally been covered . . . beyond that
the legislature should not circumscribe the exercise
of judicial authority in these cases.[14]

In 1915 the state legislature repealed all past juvenile
court legislation and passed a comprehensive juvenile court
statute that prevailed until 1961. The new act maintained juvenile court wardship over youths younger than age twenty-one ad-
judged on the basis of the fifteen "dependent" criteria cited
earlier as part of the 1909 legislation. However, the 1915 act
did not provide distinctions between delinquent, dependent, or
neglected children.

Of particular significance were the vast range of juvenile
court jurisdiction generated by statute and the lack of directives
to guide the counties in implementing juvenile court law. This
broad legislation resulted in "divergent evolution"[15] of county
juvenile court services. The divergent evolution is exemplified
in the different forms and uses of probation, detention, and probation committees among counties.

## Search for Uniformity in Juvenile Court Services

California's attempts to standardize local juvenile court
services were characterized by a service approach. This service
approach was initiated by the Board of Charities and Corrections
and continued by its successors the Department of Welfare and the
Youth Authority. No attempt was made to gain county uniformity
through legal intervention before 1961. The activities of the
State Board of Charities and Corrections and the Department of
Welfare were based on the conviction that communication would
lead to common agreement (consensus). Lemert writes:

Both the Board of Charities and Corrections and
its successor, the Department of Welfare, leaned
heavily on individual contacts, and local and state
conferences and institutes, in their search for a
common foundation of practice among those administering the juvenile court law. Behind these methods lay
a conviction that discussion would lead to a working
consensus, which would cause judges and probation officers to modify day to day operations in line with
objectives outlined in the law.[16]

The Youth Authority, had, but never exercised, formal authority over county yearly court reports and local detention and
probation practices. Like its predecessors, the Youth Authority
relied on a service approach.

The following discussion focuses on the service approach
taken by the Board of Charities and Corrections, the Department of

Welfare, and the Youth Authority in their attempts to gain county uniformity.

The State Board of Charities and Corrections, in its first attempt to assess county juvenile court and probation practices, gathered county probation statistics. The board wanted to make county comparisons, but the statistics were either inadequate or nonexistent.[17] During this period the board found wide variations in probation committee activities and noted the absence of committees in ten counties. Further variations were evident in county uses of detention. In response to these county variations the Board instituted Probation Letters to provide a medium through which probation officers could be informed of the probation activities of other counties. In addition, the board compiled information on county detention practices and found that fifty-four counties detained juveniles in some way. Forms of detention included boarding homes (twenty-two counties), specially designed detention homes (sixteen counties), county hospitals (nine counties), and subsidized homes (six counties). One county shared the detention home of an adjoining county.[18] The board subsequently made a more comprehensive study of nine counties to determine whether detention homes were necessary and, if so, what their functions should be. As a result of this survey, the board's adopted detention home standards to be used in state "approval" of detention homes and practices.

The Department of Welfare assumed responsibility for county juvenile court services in 1929. The approach followed by the Department of Welfare was similar to that of the state board. Local compliance with state laws and recommended standards was expected to be accomplished through communication. The Department of Welfare continued to organize local and statewide conferences for discussion of problems in court services and practices and search for mutually acceptable solutions. The Probation News, a monthly journal, was begun during this period to provide miscellaneous news for probation officers. Lemert describes the content and significance of this publication in the following statement:

> Communication with probation officers was further amplified through the monthly publication of Probation News. This proved to be little more than a bulletin whose news items and comments were pervaded by the values and ideology espoused in the rising field of social work. At the same time, the News struck a much more legalistic note than was true in the older Charities and Corrections Board reports. The attention of probation officers was regularly directed to appellate court decisions and Attorney General opinions bearing on the juvenile court and occasionally the items took sharp, didactic form, more or less instructing workers on procedures required by law.[19]

Some dominant areas of concern during this period were separate detention facilities for youths, no detention without court order, closed hearings for youths, and submission of annual reports by county probation committees.

Despite the lack of conformity and, in some instances, blatant violations, the Department of Welfare did not take any legal action against noncomplying counties.

In the middle 1930's an attempt was made to initiate a state system of probation to overcome the county disparities in probation practices. Ultimately, the proposal was discarded because of county-state jurisdictional disputes. Smaller counties were not at all amenable to a plan that would diminish their sovereignty. Their opposition prevented state legislation, so juvenile court and probation practices continued to be essentially county-determined.[20]

California's attempts to standardize juvenile court and probation practices decreased with the depression years and the country's subsequent entry into World War II. It has been suggested that during this time America began its move toward an administrative state. Indicators included takeover of many local welfare services by the federal and state governments and sweeping economic changes.[21] California's development of a state youth authority in 1941 was an example of the administrative trend in government.

The legislation that established the California Youth Authority was enacted in 1941. This legislation, the Youth Correction Authority Act, was patterned after the American Law Institutes' Model Youth Correction Authority Act. Robert Smith states that while "coming closer than any subsequent Youth Authority Act in other states, the California legislation did not achieve the model structure envisioned by ALI."[22] Smith points out further that both the model act and the California act were "natural responses to the social demands being exerted in 1940 and 1941, urging that something be done about justice for youth."[23]

In compliance with the 1941 legislation, the Governor appointed a three person commission (the Youth Authority). The commission's duty was essentially to submit state-committed youth (ages sixteen to twenty-three) to examination to determine and subsequently render treatment. Type of treatment could vary from prison to release under supervision. Section 1700 of the California Welfare and Institutions Code specified the Youth Authority was to be a more effective protector of society by replacing retributive punishment with training and treatment directed toward the correction and rehabilitation of youthful offenders. In effect, California's establishment of the Youth Authority was a substantial move toward administrative justice for youth.

Shortly after establishment of the Youth Authority there were two suicides and a number of runaway incidents at the Whittier State School for Boys. This particular institution had experienced seven different superintendents in one year. In addition to Whittier, there were periodic difficulties with the other two state youth correctional schools.[24]  Public concern and pressure over these incidents, including an Assembly Interim Committee investigation, led Governor Warren to request the Youth Authority to assume management of the state's three youth reformatories and juvenile parole services.  In 1943 the legislature confirmed the Youth Authority's responsibility for these institution functions.  Subsequent amendments assigned the Youth Authority limited duties and control in connection with county juvenile court and probation standards and practices.  Some of these duties included setting detention and probation standards, inspecting juvenile halls (detention facilities) and county camps receiving state subsidy, and requiring annual probation reports from counties.  The penalties for nonconforming counties were never specified and the Youth Authority never asserted formal authority over counties for noncompliance.

The Youth Authority, in similar fashion to the early state board and welfare department, relied on conferences and statewide committee meetings to gain county uniformity in detention and probation practices.  Typically, recommendations that arose from these conferences were compiled and distributed to each county.  Smith cites a particular problem between the Youth Authority and counties that was resolved by a conference.  In 1955 county juvenile court judges and Youth Authority officials were brought together to discuss the excessive county detention (one to six months) of youths awaiting state reformatory placement.  Subsequently, many judges began to grant probation in cases that previously would have resulted in a state reformatory commitment. As a result, the Youth Authority found its reformatories with empty beds and had to modify the policy.[25]

Beyond the use of conferences and committees, the Youth Authority's Field Services Division conducted initial surveys on a wide range of county activities pertaining to youths including law enforcement, schools, recreation, traffic courts, juvenile court, and probation.[26]  Generally, Youth Authority consultants were brought in by the counties to assist them in dealing with their court service related problems.  According to a probation officer, "The Youth Authority's Field Services used a consultant service method.  They assisted us with our problems, they were not an edict-issuing agency, they did not try to shove practices down our throats."  This probation officer cited his county's decision to construct a larger detention facility in the late 1940's.  The county questioned what sort of services should be included in a detention facility.  A Youth Authority detention consultant, Ray Studt, recommended to the county that, in addition to a lock-up facility, the detention center include school, counseling, and medical and psychological diagnostic services.  In this way the Youth Authority not only provided a needed service to the county but was able to recommend its standards in an unofficial and cooperative manner.

The Youth Authority's role with county juvenile court and probation practices, while similar to the two previous state agencies in approach, was improved because of greater staff, financial, and other resources.

Most of the Youth Authority's staff was drawn from either Los Angeles or Alameda counties. Given the unclear state legislation, it is not surprising that the probation standards developed by the Youth Authority strongly reflected Los Angeles and Alameda county practices.[27] Furthermore, most Youth Authority personnel had social work backgrounds, a fact that was reflected in their encouraging case work techniques in probation practice.

Chad McFarlan, a retired Youth Authority consultant, states that the Youth Authority took a gradual, one-step-at-a-time approach in its attempt to secure consensus in county juvenile court and probation practices. "We were realistic and recognized the reluctance of the counties to be dictated to by the state. Therefore, we relied on the setting example and persuasion approach," McFarlan said. The Youth Authority recognized that local probation officers came from a diversity of backgrounds (law enforcement, business, religion, etc.) and that uniformity could not be expected without developing a series of county contacts and relying on county "experiences." The Youth Authority consultants felt that as the counties experienced difficulties they would, with Youth Authority assistance, reach consensus on "appropriate" local court services and practices.

In addition to the Youth Authority's belief in eventual county consensus through experience, the strong sense of "localism" (self determination) in state politics was not taken lightly. The state senate had strong rural representation and "home rule" was felt to be a right of local government. As McFarlan points out: "The people of Humbolt County did not want Los Angeles rammed down their throats. Los Angeles' needs and problems with youth were not the same as Humbolt County's."

The Youth Authority attempted to deal with this strong "localism" sentiment through a gradual step-by-step "upgrading" process. Youth Authority Director Karl Holton and especially his successor Heman Stark felt the counties in time would share the state's ideas about court services and probation practices. Stark's successful public relations approach with the County Probation Officers Association is widely acknowledged. He established strong working relationships with the probation leaders across the state. McFarlan feels the probation officers thought his motives were good and he was not seeking state control over county court and probation functions. He credits this perception as contributing toward more ready acceptance by local authorities of state-sponsored court and probation programs.

During the late 1940's and early 1950's the Youth Authority studied court services in individual counties. As described earlier, these surveys were broad inquiries primarily concerned with law enforcement and probation problems. Stark used these surveys to further the Youth Authority's attempt to reach uniformity in county court services and gain Youth Authority credibility with counties as a "service" agency oriented toward local assistance rather than control. In the county under study, for example, this process began with a meeting between the probation officer, Stark, and Youth Authority consultants to discuss the survey findings and to work out any areas of disagreement. Following this meeting, the Youth Authority assisted the probation officer in bargaining with local interest groups to gain the county Board of Supervisors' approval and allocation of funds for the court service needs identified in the survey.

Another method the Youth Authority used to gain consensus in court and probation practices was state subsidization. State subsidy programs were considered first by the Department of Welfare in the 1930's. However, the department could not overcome strong "localism" sentiments and fear of ultimate state control and subsidy did not materialize at that time. Counties were not interested in programs that carried the possibility of state interference in county government. Like federal grants in aid, state subsidy was directed toward initiating development of specific local services in exchange for financial allocations. The first Youth Authority subsidy was made in 1945. This program encouraged county development of local institutions as alternatives to state reformatories for problem youths. Counties that received subsidies were subject to Youth Authority regulation of local youth institutions.

The subsidy approach that ultimately was accepted by most California counties will be discussed in detail in Chapters 3 and 4.

## Ambiguity of County Juvenile Court Services

Changes in California's juvenile court law from 1903 to 1961 can be described as halting steps aimed at achieving local policy uniformity and the legalizing practices already in effect locally. This pattern of reactive legislation amounted to state approval of county solutions to local problems. However, the juvenile court legislation was responsive primarily to the problems of the larger counties - Los Angeles, San Francisco and Alameda. This urban bias contributed to smaller counties resisting the law or interpreting it in a way that met their own needs.

The Youth Authority ultimately realized that--in addition to consultant services, state-wide conferences, and distribution of probation publications and research findings--other approaches were needed to move local juvenile court systems in particular programmatic directions. As a result, the subsidy approach was undertaken and has achieved the greatest amount of success to date in the state's attempts to influence local development of specific court services and program practices.

In summary, California county court service administrators, lacking clear legal directives and corresponding knowledge and financial bases, have responded primarily to local needs and second to state court and probation trends supported by significant state financing for their implementation. Therefore, determination of county juvenile court services has been a product of administrative adaptations and exchanges between local and state organizations. The nature of these organization adaptations and exchanges between local and state organizations and more recently federal organizations will be explored in the subsequent chapters.

Early County Juvenile Court and Probation Experience

In 1909 the county under study appointed a prominent local industrialist as its first probation officer to serve the courts part-time and handle both children and adult cases granted probation by the courts. From 1909 to 1927 the county's juvenile court services consisted of a juvenile court judge, a part-time probation officer, and a part-time detention facility within the county hospital's mental ward. Delinquents and dependents were not separated except in instances of overcrowding, when delinquents frequently were transferred and held in the county jail.

In 1927 the county appointed a local minister as its first full-time probation officer. In addition, a small detention facility was constructed on the county hospital grounds to house twelve dependent, neglected, or delinquent youths. However, most delinquent youths still were held in the county jail. They were held there primarily because of the small detention home capacity and the increasing number of youths detained in the county. In 1934 a part-time woman probation assistant was appointed to handle girls' and women's cases.

In interviews the juvenile court judge who served the county from 1936 to 1946 suggested that before the late 1930's the county classified problem children into two categories. "A child was either 'bad' enough to go to a state reformatory or 'good' enough to remain at home."[28] This resulted in two types of dispositions either a state reformatory commitment or home supervision.

In the late 1930's and the subsequent war years the county's probation personnel and detention facility were substantially overburdened. In 1940 the probation staff was equal to that of 1927. This included the probation officer, an assistant, a clerk, and three detention home personnel. The juvenile court judge reflected back on this era as a period in which the county was inundated by a rural southern population that became employed in the shipyards. The population of the county's major city jumped from 25,000 in 1941 to more than 100,000 by 1943. The judge stated, "there was an awful lot of immorality, a great deal of incest between father and daughters, stealing was a common practice despite the higher than usual shipyard salaries, and truancy was rampant." Many of the county's schools were on a four shift schedule and, the judge reasoned, kids had nothing else to do but get into trouble.

In response to the rising number of youths in trouble and

their immoral homes, as determined by the juvenile court, the county abandoned its previous reliance on the two category disposition system. Private institutions and foster home placements were developed and used frequently. The private institutions, with the exception of the Salvation Army Boys and Girls' Home, were Catholic sponsored youth homes. Because of a lag in state reformatory construction the Youth Authority was not a major placement source for the county.

Following the war years, the county expected a significant decrease in youths requiring court services. However, this decrease did not materialize. In 1946 there was a slight drop in petitions filed on dependent and delinquent youths and a small drop in the total number of youths admitted to detention, while the number of youths under home supervision remained constant. However, the number of juvenile court orders increased from 801 in 1945 to 1,109 in 1946. It was assumed by the county probation department that there was a beginning trend of increases in the number of youths requiring services. As a result department expansions were recommended. The following selection from the county's 1946 Annual Probation Report reflects the contemporary thinking:

> . . . it was supposed by many that there would be a great falling off in juvenile delinquency in the county. Judging from what has happened during the first two months of the current year, it would seem that the juvenile problem is definitely and steadily becoming greater.

The report went on to argue for several specific needs. As the report states, "our greatest and most pressing need is for a new juvenile hall." In addition, it was felt more probation staff and psychiatric services were required.

The current county probation officer, who assumed the position in 1946, claims that the first major development in the county's juvenile court services occurred with the construction of a new juvenile hall. The hall development won the Board of Supervisors' approval only after the county juvenile court judge bargained with a particular property owner and was able to secure the needed land for the new hall at two-thirds its market value. A Youth Authority consultant assisted the county in the juvenile hall architecture and service planning. This is reflected in the following acknowledgment by the county that is drawn from the 1950 Annual Probation Report:

> A close working relationship has been continued between Juvenile Hall and the Detention Consultant for the California Youth Authority. The Consultant assisted in a statistical survey of the length of periods of detention for delinquent and neglected children. The Juvenile Hall Superintendent was affiliated with a group of near-by juvenile hall superintendents who met monthly with the Youth Authority

Consultant. These sessions and visits to other juvenile halls offered opportunities for the exchange
of ideas on various phases of juvenile hall work.

The hall also included custodial facilities, school, counseling,
medical, and psychiatric diagnostic services. Construction was
completed in 1949 and the hall began operation in 1950.

Between 1950 and 1951 the court's probation case loads increased 15.4 percent, new juvenile referrals rose from 1,324 to
1,890 and juvenile hall admissions jumped from 1,110 to 1,526. Of
particular significance was that fifty percent of the youths detained at juvenile hall were awaiting state reformatory placements.
Such action required an average three-month wait in juvenile hall.
In response to this detention problem the county began to bargain
locally for a county operated training facility (as it was referred to in 1951). In the next chapter consideration and analysis of the local bargaining and the state's role in the county's
development of a boys' residential treatment center will be presented.

In summary, California county juvenile court and probation
systems were relatively free to respond to perceived local needs
in their development of services. For example, the county under
study developed its juvenile court services from 1909 to 1950
primarily in response to changing functional necessities (i.e.:
increasing numbers of youths coming into contact with the court
and corresponding local accommodations (i.e.: the purchase of
land for the juvenile hall at a substantially discounted price).
The state juvenile court law was of little assistance to county
administrators in their development of juvenile court services.
The Youth Authority's field consulting service was significant in
the final outcome of the detention facility. However, the Youth
Authority did not have substantial influence on any other probation activities or court service developments in the county until
the 1950's, when the 1945 camp, ranch, and school subsidy was revised.

[1] David J. Rothman, _The Discovery of the Asylum_ (1971), pp. 82-83.

[2] Anthony M. Platt, _The Child Savers_ (1969), p. 53.

[3] Rothman, _The Discovery of the Asylum_, p. 209.

[4] Preston School of Industry, Fourth Biennal Report of the Board of Trustees (1898-1900), p. 17.

[5] For an interesting discussion of the differential or special handling of youthful offenders prior to juvenile courts see Platt, _The Child Savers_, pp. 183-202.

[6] Platt, _The Child Savers_, pp. 137-145.

[7] Edwin Lemert, _Social Action and Legal Change_ (1970), p. 37.

[8] Frances Cahn and Valeska Bary, _Welfare Activities of Federal, State and Local Governments in California 1850-1934_ (1936), p. 72.

[9] Cahn and Bary, _Welfare Activities of Federal, State, and Local Governments in California 1850-1934_, p. 73.

[10] Cahn and Bary, _Welfare Activities of Federal, State, and Local Governments in California 1850-1934_, p. 73.

[11] Cahn and Bary, _Welfare Activities of Federal, State, and Local Governments in California 1850-1934_, p. 74.

[12] Cahn and Bary, _Welfare Activities of Federal, State, and Local Governments in California 1850-1934_, p. 73.

[13] Lemert, _Social Action and Legal Change_, pp. 23 and 40.

[14] _Transactions of the Commonwealth Club of California_ Vol. V. (San Francisco, 1910), p. 248.

[15] See Lemert, _Social Action and Legal Change_, pp. 41-46.

[16] Lemert, _Social Action and Legal Change_, p. 47.

[17] Cahn and Bary, _Welfare Activities of Federal, State, and Local Governments in California 1850-1934_, p. 78.

[18] Cahn and Bary, _Welfare Activities of Federal, State, and Local Governments in California 1850-1934_, p. 81.

[19] Lemert, _Social Action and Legal Change_, pp. 47-48.

[20] Lemert, _Social Action and Legal Change_, p. 49.

21Lemert, Social Action and Legal Change, p. 49.

22Robert Lee Smith, "Youth and Correction: An Institutional Analysis of the California Youth Authority," (Unpublished Masters Thesis, Berkeley, University of California, 1955), p. 6.

23Smith, "Youth and Correction: An Institutional Analysis of the California Youth Authority," p. 6.

24Unpublished historical account of California Youth Authority by William Underwood, Consultant, Department of the Youth Authority, Division of Delinquency Prevention and Probation Services, February, 1968.

25Smith, "Youth and Correction: An Institutional Analysis of the California Youth Authority," p. 64.

26Lemert, Social Action and Legal Change, p. 57.

27The information on the Youth Authority's relationship with county probation departments was drawn from a number of interviews. The major source of information was C. H. McFarlan, a Youth Authority County Consultant under directors Karl Holton, Heman Stark, and Allan Breed.

28The County's Juvenile Court Judge from 1936 to 1946 is currently a State Justice in the Court of Appeals, he is also a past president of the California Probation, Parole, and Correctional Officers Association.

CHAPTER 3


BOYS'TREATMENT CENTER:  A LOCAL INSTITUTION
ALTERNATIVE TO STATE REFORMATORIES


This chapter focuses on:  (1) Youth Authority and county conditions that lead to the quest for a local treatment institution (boys' center, hereafter), (2) state and local organization bargaining and exchange required for development of the boys' center, and (3) operation and inpact of boys' center.  The chapter includes sections describing the Youth Authority and county court services before the boys' center; the Camp, Ranch, and School Subsidy Acts of 1945 and 1957; and the local political campaign for the boys' center.

Central issues to be investigated include organization dynamics involved in a comparison of the boys' center development and the local court perception of the boys' center's function with the state's expectations for local instituions.


## Pre-Treatment Center Setting

California Youth Authority was established in 1941.  Within a decade the state's total population had increased fifty percent.  During this period the state's youth reformatory population almost doubled, moving from 1,300 in 1941 to 2,526 in 1953.  Before 1965, when the Youth Authority implemented probation subsidy to decrease county commitments of youth to state reformatories, the state's response to increased commitments had been to build more institutions.  However, during World War II and the early 1950's, there were lags in state reformatory construction while county commitments to state reformatories continued to climb.  The results, in the early 1950's, were long local detention waits (three to six months) for youths pending reformatory placement.

The increase in county commitments to state reformatories has been attributed to conflicting ideas between the state and counties on the appropriate use of state institutions.  Counties believed Youth Authority reformatories provided greater treatment opportunities and more security than did local probation programs.[1]  In contrast, Karl Holton, Youth Authority director from 1941 until 1952, attributed frequent commitment of youths to state reformatories to "erroneous attitudes" on the part of county judges.[2]  His feelings, as well as those of Stark (Youth Authority director in 1952), were that state reformatories were the appropriate alternative only after all local efforts had failed.  In an attempt to solve this county-state conflict, Governor's Conferences on Children and Youth were held in 1948, 1950, and 1954.  These conferences, instigated by the Youth Authority, found that many children were being held in detention unnecessarily. In 1952, a special study about county detention and child care was conducted for the Governor's Children and Youth Committee. The study determined that 41 percent of the state's entire detention population was being held without justification. The study further pointed out that, in relation to national averages, California was detaining the highest percentage of its arrested youth.

With no state reformatory openings or local institution alternatives, counties began using their juvenile halls (detention facilities) for multiple functions.[3] This action resulted in a severe overloading of local detention facilities and many counties became involved in significant controversies over the detention issue. In a 1958 survey by the Governor's Juvenile Justice Commission it was concluded that twenty-eight percent of California's probation officers believed detention to be therapeutically valuable and forty percent of the juvenile court judges felt detention was justified to insure a child's appearance in court.[4] Those who opposed the treatment or insurance-of-court-appearance rationales for detention argued that detention was not the time or the place for treatment and that citations would work just as well to insure a child's appearance in court.[5]

The detention issue dates back to California's early juvenile court acts and amendments. Despite the persistence of this issue, clear detention guidelines for counties to follow were not formulated until 1960. The Youth Authority, true to its service tradition, did attempt to influence local detention practices by providing counties special detention consultants and arranging conferences where a number of juvenile hall superintendents would meet and exchange detention ideas. In addition, Holton and Stark encouraged the statewide surveys to illustrate detention abuses and disparities.

The county under study began operation of its new juvenile hall in 1950. The new facility increased the county's detention capacity from twenty-seven to eighty children. In the 1950 Annual Probation Report the purpose and admission criteria of the hall were stated as follows:

> Its function is to provide short term care for children who come under the jurisdiction of the Juvenile Court. These include delinquent and neglected children who cannot safely, from the standpoint of their own or community welfare, be left at home pending disposition of their cases by the Juvenile Court. Juvenile Hall is not a penal or correctional institution. In accordance with the law, as well as the policies and programs of the department, Juvenile Hall is operated as nearly as possible in a homelike fashion. A conscientious effort is made by the department to admit for detention or shelter only those children whose needs and problems require that they be in Juvenile Hall.

In 1950 as earlier mentioned, the juvenile hall admitted a total of 1,110 youths compared to 927 in 1949, and 904 in 1948. In 1951 juvenile hall admissions jumped to 1,526 with a daily population average of 75.4, a 28.7 percent increase from the 1950 daily average. The county estimated that twenty-five to fifty percent of the youths were awaiting state reformatory placements, which resulted in three month detention waits after court appearance. In response to the significant increase in the juvenile hall population, the probation department began to argue for a local "treatment" institution as an alternative to state reformatory commitments and the accompanying long detention waits. The 1951 Annual Probation Report argued:

> At the present time from twenty-five percent to fifty percent of the boys detained at the Juvenile Hall are waiting to be delivered to a State Training School. Each boy committed waits about three months in Juvenile Hall after his court appearance. If it were possible to move these boys out of Juvenile Hall immediately after commitment, the detention load would be considerably lightened. The best method of solving this problem is to provide a county operated training facility for boys where the majority of them could be sent immediately.

From 1952 through 1956 the county's juvenile hall population and state reformatory commitments stabilized. Although the actual figures in 1952 to 1956 were higher than those in the late 1940's and early 1950's, the annual percentage increase had subsided (see Tables 1 and 2). However, by June of 1953 the juvenile court's probation department had successfully convinced local political interests and the County Board of Supervisors of the need for a local institution to handle the rising numbers of troubled youth.

The county was concerned with reducing its detention load when the Boys' Center development was initiated. The probation officer summarized, "there was a major detention problem associated with the backlog of boys awaiting state reformatory placements. Furthermore, the county was growing fast and it was anticipated that this growth would continue."[6] To overcome both the immediate backlog and projected rising number of youth contacts and the associated organization problems, the probation department sought to expand itself through the development of the Boys' Center. Thus, the Boys' Center emerged not in direct response to youth needs but as an organization-centered response to local facility overcrowding and an external (state) funding opportunity. Here the difference between organization- and client-centered change essentially was one of expansion for probation organization maintenance needs versus change directly connected with the explicit treatment needs of troubled youths.

TABLE 1

YEARLY JUVENILE HALL ADMISSIONS, DAILY AVERAGE
POPULATION AND YEARLY STATE REFORMATORY COMMITMENTS[7]

| Year | Juvenile Hall | | State Reformatory- Number of Commitments |
| | Yearly Admissions | Daily Average Population | |
|------|------------------|-------------------------|------------------------------------------|
| 1944 | 789 | 21.2 | |
| 1945 | 932 | 25.0 | 32 |
| 1946 | 911 | 30.6 | 15 |
| 1947 | 849 | 39.7 | 21 |
| 1948 | 904 | 49.4 | 20 |
| 1949 | 927 | 49.8 | 30 |

TABLE 2

YEARLY JUVENILE HALL ADMISSIONS, DAILY AVERAGE
POPULATION AND YEARLY STATE REFORMATORY COMMITMENTS

| Year | Juvenile Hall | | State Reformatory- Number of Commitments |
| | Yearly Admissions | Daily Average Population | |
|------|------------------|-------------------------|------------------------------------------|
| 1950 | 1,110 | 46.7 | 25 |
| 1951 | 1,527 | 75.4 | 22 |
| 1952 | 1,585 | 74.2 | 43 |
| 1953 | 1,799 | 75.5 | 63 |
| 1954 | 1,787 | 74.0 | 51 |
| 1955 | 1,653 | 74.6 | 80 |
| 1956 | 1,727 | 86.1 | 51 |

History of California's Camp, Ranch, and School Subsidy Acts

County correction institutions for youth, as they now exist
in California, began in Los Angeles County in 1932, although San
Francisco used "Training Ship, Jamestown" for the rehabilitation
of problem youths in the 1870's. A Los Angeles County camp was

34

established to cope with transient youth who were said to be coming to the Los Angeles area in great numbers during the depression. The following statement provides an amusing appraisal of this period in Los Angeles:

> In 1932, depression-ridden, transient boys were coming to Los Angeles in great numbers. Available detention facilities were filled to maximum capacities. Continuing arrivals necessitated the returning of the boys to their 'point of origin' at county expense. Transients throughout the Nation learned: 'If you ride the rods out to California, they will send you home on the cushions.' Several amusing incidents illustrate the not-so-amusing problem: One small boy, it is recalled, promised the judge to return and stay home in Indiana if he would be allowed to see his favorite motion-picture star in person. The judge, in an indulgent mood, made arrangements and the boy not only met his favorite 'cowboy' but was allowed to ride the actor's famous horse. A month later the boy returned to California and appeared again before the judge, this time with three other transient companions. The boy explained to the judge: 'You see, judge, my friends didn't believe I met him (the cowboy). They want to ride on his horse, too.' Another boy, from the deep South, listened to the judge remark: 'This is the third and last time I am going to see you in this court.' 'What's the matter, judge,' the boy responded questionably, 'you going to quit?'

> To discourage the arrival of these transient children the Board of Supervisors met in special session and approved a plan to establish temporary work camps to help them earn passage home. The plan carried the endorsement of the judge of the juvenile court, the probation officer, and the county forester and fire warden.[8]

The Los Angeles camps involved the joint supervision of youths by juvenile court probation officers and county forestry employees. The program was felt to be successful and California enacted legislation in 1935 authorizing other California counties to establish forestry camps based on the Los Angeles program.[9]

In 1945 there were eleven county operated probation camps in California. During this year, California enacted legislation entitled "Juvenile Homes" that provided state maintenance and operation subsidies to encourage counties to develop local treatment institutions. The legislation included the stipulation that the Youth Authority would prescribe minimum construction and operation standards. However, between 1945 and 1957 only five new county institutions for juveniles were constructed[10] (see Table 3). Chad McFarlan points out that before the subsidy program in 1945, the state Department of Welfare had considered subsidizing counties

TABLE 3

THE DEVELOPMENT OF COUNTY TREATMENT
INSTITUTIONS IN CALIFORNIA FOR JUVENILES
1945-1970

| Year | Number of Facilities | Youth Capacity |
|---|---|---|
| 1945 | 11 | 690 |
| 1955-56 | 16 | 975 |
| 1960-61 | 31 | 2,000 |
| 1962-63 | 41 | 2,800 |
| 1964-65 | 42 | 2,894 |
| 1966-67 | 50 | 3,082 |
| 1968-69 | 54 | 3,476 |
| 1969-70 | 68 | 3,677 |

for particular court service developments to achieve greater
standardization in county juvenile court practices.  However,
the welfare department had concluded that subsidies could not
overcome the strong localism and county fears of state takeover.
According to McFarlan, "the counties were not ready for it.  They
did not want any level of state authority such as that which
would accompany state subsidization."

In 1957 the legislature increased the camp subsidy to include matching state funds for construction, as well as operation
and maintenance, of county camps or ranches.  Counties could
qualify for the Camp, Ranch, and School Subsidy of 1957 by meeting the following general criteria:

1.  Be established by county ordinance, pursuant to
    Section 881, Welfare and Institutions Code.

2.  Have in residence only juvenile court wards on
    commitment by the juvenile court.

3.  Establish a treatment-oriented program designed
    for children committed for a minimum of thirty
    consecutive days.

4.  Have an identifiable geographic area and programs
    that are physically separated from other county
    institutions or programs.

5.  Employ separate staff responsible to the super-
    intendent of the juvenile home, ranch or camp.

Within four years the number of county operated youth treatment institutions increased from sixteen to thirty-one.  During

the next ten years, from 1960 to 1970, thirty-seven additional county treatment facilities were constructed.

The 1957 camp, ranch, and school subsidy revision resulted from a decision by Stark, then director of the Youth Authority, that an increased financial incentive would encourage counties to develop local camps, ranches, or treatment institutions.  Stark said he arrived at this opinion after a series of meetings with the Probation Advisory Committee (a group of California probation officers) and many individual discussions with probation officers.

In interviews about Stark's approach in encouraging counties to develop camps and ranches, Robert L. Smith and Robert Craft[11] indicated "the Probation Advisory Committee served as a sounding board for new ideas or programs pertaining to juvenile court services."  Stark attempted to gain county consensus by first "throwing out" the camp idea at general meetings.  This action was followed by individual discussions in which Stark put forth the question, "if we could provide a new subsidy, could and would you then build county institutions?"  The decision to include construction costs in the subsidy act, was made after probation officers indicated their difficulty in obtaining substantial county funds for probation  program developments.  Therefore, before the 1957 camp, ranch, and school subsidy revision was proposed formally, the Youth Authority and probation officers from a number of counties had agreed that if construction funds were made available local probation departments would be in a much stronger position to gain matching county funds for camps or ranches.  Stark's initial conception of subsidy necessitated preliminary bargaining and minimal state and county concensus.  Smith and Craft pointed out that subsidy without these prior conditional agreements would have been "like putting the money on a stump and running like hell."

The bargaining between Stark and the county probation officers was another step toward developing state and county consensus on the county institution issue.  This effort involved negotiations that resulted in conditional reciprocal or exchange agreements.  The conditional agreement was that if increased state subsidy was available the county probation departments would push for the necessary local support to initiate county institution development.  Stark was well known for his ability to secure legislative approval for various Youth Authority programs and expansions and, therefore, many county probation departments began their campaigns for local support even before legislative approval of the revised subsidy.

Craft believes Stark's probation background influenced the Youth Authority push for the expansion of county probation institutions during the 1950's.  Stark's probation career began in Los Angeles county probation camps.  Throughout his years as director of the Youth Authority, Stark was known as a believer in county-based corrections.  He clung to the idea that the best way to deal with problem youths was through community-based treatment.  He felt this treatment could best be accomplished through the expan-

37

sion of county juvenile court services.

A more comprehensive explanation of the Youth Authority's advancement of county probation expansion, according to Smith, lies in a contradiction of Youth Authority goals and interests. The original thrust of the Youth Authority was in research, development, and upgrading of community correction services for youth. However, because of major problems in the state's reformatories in 1942 (superintendent turnover, well-publicized suicides, and frequent runaways), the Governor requested and the legislature confirmed the Youth Authority to manage the state's reformatories and their parole services. This development brought about what Smith terms "a contradiction of interests" that explains why the Youth Authority would in 1957 advocate county institution expansion that could, in fact, undermine the state's reformatory functions. It is significant that because of indirect (delay in state reformatory placements) and direct (camp, ranch, and school subsidy) influences by the Youth Authority, the county probation department developed a serious commitment to a local institution program. This began to move the department from relatively straight-forward probation services - providing social histories for the court and informally and formally supervising cases granted probation - to a full scale county level correctional establishment.

## Role of Local Groups in Boys' Treatment Center Development

Local bargaining for a county youth treatment facility began with an argument when the probation department pushed for a new detention facility. The argument, which appeared in the county's 1946 Annual Probation Report, was:

> At present, there is no in-between facility available to which delinquent boys twelve years of age and over can be committed. They must be in their own homes, on probation or with the California Youth Authority. Although most youth admitted there would be returned home after a period of five to ten days, the program should be planned so that some children could remain there from four to six months . . . A very satisfactory site has been located and the Board of Supervisors has been requested to buy it. The matter is under consideration by the Board of Supervisors. Service clubs and women's groups are interesting themselves in this problem. It is believed that they will strongly support this move.

Between 1945 and 1952 the county experienced increasing difficulty in placing court wards in state reformatories after court disposition. This problem was reflected in increased daily population in the juvenile hall (see Tables 1 and 2). In addition, the county was committing more youths to state reformatories which is also reflected in Tables 1 and 2.

These court and probation department difficulties were acknowledged by both the County Superior Court Judges Committee and the County Probation Committee (later to be called Juvenile Justice Commission). Support of these two county organizations was sought before any other local support. The county probation officer explained, "if you had a probation problem that involved county financing, you needed the joint support of all the judges. Therefore, you go to the judges first and air your case." The judges, who appoint the probation committee, carry a lot of influence and if they are in agreement with the probation officer, the probation committee is likely to agree as well.

The probation officer summarized the process as one in which "you always go through the appropriate channels. If you don't, you will be labeled an empire builder and ultimately lose your constituency. You have to learn how the bureaucracy works. I have been criticized because I am not aggressive enough but there are times that you can take advantage of opportunities if you have not developed enemies. You must be able to expand or contract depending on the political circumstances or need at hand."

Between 1945 and 1952 the probation officer was able to establish consensus between the county's judges and probation committee about the need for a boys' treatment center. The question in 1952 was how to secure broader local support. In a joint meeting of the Superior Court Judges Committee, probation committee and the county probation officer it was decided that a citizens' committee, set up to study the county's need for a treatment institution, would be an appropriate strategy. It was further determined that there were several local groups that would support this type of development and that, in addition, carried political influence with the County Board of Supervisors.

The Citizens' Committee membership included the county probation officer, the juvenile court judge, a probation committee member, the assistant superintendent of schools, a representative of the county's Federation of Women's Clubs, and the president of the county's PTA district. The county probation officer stated, "people were selected whose name meant something to the Board of Supervisors." The probation officer said the PTA president was chosen because of her known political influence and interest in the boys' center. The women's groups had a history of supporting court service expansions. This support was based on the assumption that more services would lead to declines in county youth problems, according to the probation officer. Thus, these groups were normally sought out by the probation department when department expansions were proposed. The assistant superintendent of schools, who chaired the committee, had a particular interest in the boys' center development. The county schools were dissatisfied with court response to truancy, which amounted to home-probation supervision. The county probation officer explained to school officials that serious truants should not be sent to state reformatories but could certainly be handled by the boys' center. With this service in mind, county school officials became involved in the supportive politics for the boys' center.

The Citizens' Committee activities were shaped by the probation officer. He arranged tours to selected counties that were successfully operating boys' treatment institutions. The committee visited the county's juvenile hall and were familiarized with the problematic detention conditions that were to be relieved with the addition of a local institution. In addition, the committee members who were not directly connected with probation were informed of the variety of juvenile court and probation problems. These problems included the rising number of court referrals, lack of "adequate" institution alternatives for problem youths, waiting problems associated with state reformatory commitments, the associated over-reliance on home probation supervision, and detention problems that were said to be connected with the lack of a local institution. The probation officer attempted to convince committee members of the general need for the local institution. This could best be accomplished by demonstrating the connection between the boys' center and the interests represented by the three members who were not directly connected with the court and probation.

As already mentioned, the school administrator was interested in supporting the boys' center because of its potential in deterring or institutionally treating serious truants. The PTA district had a Juvenile Protection Committee of which the probation officer was a member. This committee was directly concerned with new local youth services programs. The function of the committee was either to provide financial or, as in the case of the boys' center, political support for those youth programs it considered appropriate. Similarly, in its by-laws, the Federation of Women's Clubs specified child-welfare as one of its chief interests. This group was responsible for gathering funds for the county's first juvenile hall in 1927 and, according to the county probation officer, continually involved itself in court service developments. As earlier noted, women's groups were generally supportive of community developments for youth that they interpreted as progressive and, therefore, contributions to better community living.

In summary, the interaction between the probation officer and the various citizens' committee members involved establishing consensus for exchange in the form of subsequent political influence. While the exchange did not involve an immediate return, the member's action was directed toward either goal enhancement or the safeguard of the interests of the citizen member's organization. The citizen member's "medium of exchange" to the probation department was political influence in support of the department's quest for a new institution facility. The "medium of exchange" provided by the probation department was conditioned on the successful operation of the boys' center and in connection with both the long and short range goals and interests of the organizations that the committee members represented.

Following the successful "process of familiarization," committee members met and discussed how they should present their arguments to the County Board of Supervisors. The probation officer was successful in establishing a substantial level of "domain consensus" among the citizens' committee. Therefore, it was decided that each member would argue individually for the boys' center.  On June 9, 1953, each of the six members spoke before the County Board of Supervisors.  The Board of Supervisors responded in August by requesting from the Federal Government a county lease for facilities that once were a part of a military base.  The facilities were to be used for establishment of the boys' center.  However, the Federal Government did not respond to the lease request, which necessitated the development of another plan.

In 1955 the Board of Supervisors appropriated $30,000 with which the county was to purchase a site for a new county branch jail.  The old branch jail site was then to be turned over to the probation department for the boys' center.  This plan was found to be unsatisfactory by both the probation department and the sheriff's department.  The following year the Board of Supervisors increased the sum to $45,000 for purchase of a site specifically for the boys' center.  It was not until 1958 that the county was able to locate and purchase a satisfactory site.  The revised camp, ranch, and school subsidy was now in effect.  To qualify for funds state standards had to be met.  The county decided on a three phase construction plan.  Phase I, to be completed in 1959, would enable the county to care for twenty boys.  Phase II, in 1960, would increase the capacity to forty.  Phase III, in 1961, would complete the center with a sixty-boy capacity.

## Boys' Center Operation

In 1960 the boys' center began operation with seventeen boys.  The facility's superintendent had been a deputy probation officer with the county since 1952.  The center's staff included the superintendent, two deputy probation officers, three counselors, two cooks, and a secretary.  The center's program was described in the county's 1959 Annual Probation Report as follows:

In this initial phase the Boys' Center will offer a twenty-four hour program for twenty-one delinquent boys between the approximate ages of fourteen and sixteen years.  The program will be half a day work and half a day school with a strong emphasis on remedial education and group counseling. The Boys' Center will fill a long needed local treatment program for delinquent boys who are not able to adjust in the community and need a twenty-four hour program before further planning can be done on their behalf.  The operation of the Boys' Center should provide a reduction in the population of the younger delinquent boys section at the Juvenile Hall, where many boys have been awaiting placements ordered by the Juvenile Court.

The boys' center emphasized middle-class behavior standards such as school and work achievement, good table manners, and temper restraint.  Cussing and smoking were prohibited.  Each boy was expected to pass through a series of progressive stages and to undergo weekly evaluations by the entire staff. Therapeutic community (TC) was the principal treatment mode used at the center. Two meetings were held each day in which staff and boys would criticize each other as well as themselves. Self criticism was assumed to be essential for rehabilitation. Many staff members felt that TC meetings were tremendously successful, especially from a group-control standpoint. Most boys felt these meetings were primarily "fink-sessions" in which they were to inform the counselors about wrongdoings they had witnessed or been involved in.

In the beginning years many youths accepted to the center came from middle-class families and had demonstrated an inability to get along satisfactorily with their parents. In these cases the therapeutic community, which was a middle-class treatment mode, was not a particularly difficult one in which to adjust. However, some youths, generally minority or lower-class, experienced difficulty fitting into the center's regimentation. In many such instances the youths chose to run away. This action generally resulted in their return to juvenile hall and subsequent state reformatory commitment. The probation department pushed state reformatory commitments for boys' center runaways to discourage the practice, but despite this approach youths continued to run away. Many indicated a desire to go to state reformatories rather than the center because of their belief that "state time" was less difficult than "county time."

For client selection, the center used an intake committee. The committee was comprised of the probation department psychologist, the juvenile hall and boys' center school principal, and the center's superintendent. The intake decision process involved a presentation by a deputy probation officer. The deputy probation officer presented information on why the youth was appropriate for the center. This presentation was followed by discussion between intake committee members and probation representatives in an attempt to reach a decision with consensus.

After several months there emerged what the center's superintendent described as "an understanding" among the county's juvenile probation officers as to the type of youth that was a boys' center "client-type." This agreement is reflected in the county's 1960 Annual Probation Report, which included a description of the boys' center "client-type" after the center had been in operation less than six months. The report states:

> It seems the center's program is most helpful
> to boys whose history of delinquency does not ex-
> tend further back than two to three years. This
> type of boy seems to adapt himself more readily to
> the program and is able to gain insight into some
> of the causes contributing to his delinquency. We
> have been least helpful to the immature boy who has
> a long history of deprived emotional life. The lat-
> ter boy often has difficulty in relating to his peer

group and needs a program of much longer duration.

In summary, a central point that emerges is that as a result of indirect and direct Youth Authority influence and action, the county juvenile court and probation department developed a serious commitment to an institution program. This institution commitment began to move the department from a relatively straightforward court-assisting agency to a county level correctional establishment. This movement changed the character of the department. One index of this change is the varying distribution over time in the court services meted out to youths. This distribution will be investigated in the impact assessment of the boys' center.

## Impact Assessment

Methodology. The characteristic form of statistical evaluation in sociological research is to gather and analyze data that correspond to a theoretical model.[12] The statistical approach used in this study relies on "official" statistics to reflect patterns of activity in an organization's decision-making structure. It is assumed that decision-making patterns in juvenile court systems are, in part, a product of the court's organization structure. Based on this assumption, it is expected that when court service alternatives were added, changes will occur in court decision-making patterns. The impact of a new court service program is expected to include processes by which youths come to be defined, classified, and placed in corresponding new court service categories.[13] Placement of youths in juvenile court service categories is recorded in court and probation statistical summaries. These statistics identify specific categories and indicate how often each category is used. Therefore, by examining changes in the court organization structure (i.e.: fluctuating court service alternatives) and subsequent related statistics (i.e.: form of court control administered), patterns should emerge that can point to a connection between court decision-making and court organization.

The impact assessment to be used here and in Chapters 4 and 5 is a descriptive analysis of the county's statistical patterns several years before and several years after development of the boys' center, probation subsidy, and diversion.

The assessments begin with statistical descriptions of the county's population, juvenile arrests, court intake referrals, referrals closed at intake or placed under informal probation, petitions filed, and subsequent forms of court control. The figures for youthful population, arrests, court referrals, and petitions filed are included to account for any significant statistical fluctuation that could affect court control patterns. However, the impact of these three developments (boys' center, probation subsidy, and diversion) is examined primarily in relation to court control patterns statistically evident before and after each development had begun. The formal goals assigned to the new programs provide a frame of reference for the impact assessments.

Juvenile Justice Process Overview. Before discussing the impact assessments, it is necessary to describe the juvenile justice process from arrest to juvenile court decision. The first step usually is a youth's arrest, which can be followed by either reprimand and release by the police or a referral to county juvenile court intake. Most court intake referrals originate from the police but a child can be referred by parents, school, or other sources. Following a referral, intake personnel can release the youth, place him on informal probation without supervision, or file a petition for court action. At the juvenile court hearing the judge can dismiss the case, place the youth on six months home probation without court wardship, or arrive at a formal disposition that varies from county to county depending on available court service alternatives. Usually this includes formal supervision at home or in a foster home, county institution facilities, or state reformatories.

Boys' Center Impact. The underlying assumptions in this study is that program expansions in juvenile court services produce changes in (1) the forms of supervision provided youth and (2) the number of youths under supervision. New court service programs are expected to result in a process of new client discovery and client displacement. In client displacement a proportion of the court's cases are displaced from previously operating programs into the new program. A development such as the boys' center provides an additional institution program alternative to the juvenile court. Adding local institutions provides an enlarged institution capacity, considering both state reformatories and local institutions. It is expected that, as a result of expanded institution capacity, the proportion of delinquent boys receiving some form of institution service will increase. Increased availability of a service and subsequent client-drawing process is referred to in this study as the "program magnet phenomenon."

However, the official reason for developing the local institution was to provide an alternative to the state reformatory. Thus, the proportion of youths receiving some form of institution service in the county (i.e.: boys' center and state reformatory) should have remained fairly constant.

This chapter explores the program management phenomenon in investigating the relation between the boys' center and the court's methods of administering control to delinquent boys.

The county's 1957 Annual Probation Report contained an emphatic call for increased probation staff and a local institution for girls, and anticipated the relief the boys' center would provide in reducing the county's reliance on state reformatories for youth placement.

In Table 4, mean percentage comparisons for 1957 to 1959 (three years before the boys' center operation) and 1960 to 1962 (three years during the boys' center operation) are provided for

44

TABLE 4

COUNTY YOUTH POPULATION, ARRESTS, JUVENILE COURT INTAKE REFERRALS
OF DELINQUENT BOYS'CASES AND SUBSEQUENT DISPOSITION
OF INTAKE REFERRALS

|  | Mean | |
|---|---|---|
|  | 1957-59 | 1960-62 |
| Youthful Population Age 10-17 | 54,654 | 64,987 |
| Juvenile Arrests | 7,378 | 11,453 |
| Percent of Youthful Population | 13.5 | 17.6 |
| Juvenile Court Intake Referrals (Boys' Cases) | 1,522 | 1,836 |
| Percent of Youthful Population | 2.8 | 2.8 |
| Referrals Closed at Intake or Placed Under Informal Probation | 797 | 1,157 |
| Percent of Intake Referrals | 52.4 | 63.0 |
| Petitions Filed in Juvenile Court | 725 | 679 |
| Percent of Intake Referrals | 47.6 | 37.0 |

the county's youth population, juvenile arrests, juvenile court
intake referrals of delinquent boys' cases, cases closed at intake or placed under informal probation, and court petitions filed
on boys' cases. The percentage comparison of juvenile arrests
indicate a 4.1 percent increase and boys referral either closed at
intake or placed under informal probation increased by 10.6 percent during the 1960 to 1962 period with an equivalent percentage
decline in petitions filed. Overall these figures suggest that
the boys' cases referred to juvenile court intake during the boys'
center operation are less serious than during the three years
before the boys' center. As a result, proportionately more of the
referrals are being closed at intake or placed under informal probation and less petitions for juvenile court appearance are being
filed. The significance of the increased proportion of juvenile
arrests to boys' center operation is unclear because the arrest
data include girls. Arrest data on boys only were not available.

The yearly totals of delinquent boys under some form of
court control from 1957 to 1962 are provided in Table 5. During
the 1960 to 1962 period the average proportion of boys receiving
state reformatory control was equivalent to the 1957 to 1959

45

## TABLE 5

SUMMARY TOTALS OF DELINQUENT BOYS' CASES UNDER SOME FORM OF
JUVENILE COURT OR STATE REFORMATORY CONTROL

| | 1957 | 1958 | 1959 | 1960 | 1961 | 1962 |
|---|---|---|---|---|---|---|
| Delinquent Boys' Cases Under Control | 592 | 669 | 665 | 763 | 708 | 764 |
| Delinquent Boys' Cases Receiving Some Form of Juvenile Court Control Other than Boys' Center and State Reformatory | 533 | 610 | 600 | 690 | 601 | 661 |
| Delinquent Boys' Cases Receiving Boys' Center Control | - | - | - | 17 | 20 | 20 |
| Delinquent Boys' Cases Receiving State Reformatory Control | 59 | 59 | 65 | 56 | 87 | 83 |
| Proportion of Delinquent Cases Under State Reformatory Control | .100 | .089 | .098 | .073 | .123 | .109 |

period even though the boys' center was in operation. The 1957 to 1959 mean proportion of delinquent boys receiving state reformatory control was .10. During 1960 to 1962 the mean proportion was .10. Given the official purpose of the boys' center, it should have been expected that proportionately fewer boys would have been sent to state reformatories and placed instead into the boys' center.

Table 6 provides a percentage measurement of the change in the numbers of delinquent boys receiving state reformatory control during the first three years of the boys' center operation. Using a base expectancy rate (see note to Table 6), an expected number of boys to be under state control was computed. A comparison of the expected number with the actual number (three-year mean) resulted in no change; namely 74 expected and 75 actually receiving state reformatory control. However, a comparison using an estimated number that excludes the boys' center youths (who theoretically would have likely gone to state reformatories) with the actual number in state reformatories resulted in a 36.0 percent increase. This comparison demonstrates that, with the addition of the boys' center, boys previously judged not in need of institution control are now being judged, within a less constrained framework of institution alternatives, suitable for an institution placement. The court has increased its control over delinquent boys.

The major question that emerges from these data is whether the county's increased use of institution control reflects (1) a greater number of more serious problem boys coming before the court or (2) modification of the court's decision-making constraints resulting in more boys receiving institution control. A breakdown of reasons for delinquent boys' referrals to the court both before the boys' center and during its first three years of operation indicates that fewer boys were referred for specific offenses (602's) and more for delinquent tendencies (601's). (See Tables 7 and 8.) The delinquent tendency category generally refers to youths who have difficulty with their parents. The normal response is informal or formal home supervision and, if this fails, placement with a relative or in a foster home. Therefore, with the county's increase in boys referred for delinquent tendencies during the 1960 to 1962 period, there should have been an increase in less severe dispositions instead of the reported increase in institution placements.

Given the client composition coming before the court during the 1960 to 1962 period it can be argued that the county's pattern of control over boys probably was not in direct connection with boys' needs, but instead reflected a change in the decision-making structure of the court. Because of structural modification, a number of cases were displaced from a previous service alternative and into the new alternative, the boys' center.

A major assumption in this study is that the determination of delinquent in need of service is made, in part, by the organization alternatives available within a particular court system.

TABLE 6

COMPARISON OF AN EXPECTED AND AN ESTIMATED NUMBER OF DELINQUENT
BOYS UNDER STATE REFORMATORY CONTROL IN 1960-62 WITH ACTUAL NUM-
BER OF DELINQUENT BOYS UNDER STATE REFORMATORY CONTROL[1]

| | 1960-62 Mean of Actual Number of Boys' Under State Reforma-tory Control | Difference | Percentage Increase |
|---|---|---|---|
| Expected Number of Delinquent Boys Under Control at the State Reforma-tory: | 75      75 | | − |
| Estimated Number of Delinquent Boys Under Control at the State Reforma-tory: | 56      75 | +19 | 35.0 |

[1]To compute the expected number of delinquent boys to be
subject to state reformatory control during Boys' Center's first
three years of operation--a base expectancy rate is used.  The
base expectancy rate is a mean of the proportion of delinquent
boys' cases under some form of court control receiving state reformatory control during 1957-1959.  The expected number of boys
to be under state reformatory control is computed by multiplying
the base expectancy rate or .10 by the mean of delinquent boys'
cases under some form of court control during 1960-1962 or .745.
Additionally, an estimated number of delinquent boys to be subject to state reformatory control is provided to directly assess
the impact of the Boys' Center upon the county's use of the state
reformatory for delinquent boys.  The estimated number is computed
by subtracting the 1960-1962 mean of delinquent boys receiving
Boys'Center control (19) from the expected number of delinquent
boys to be subject to state reformatory control.

The boys' center provided an additional organization alternative
that resulted in a restructured decision-making system.  This
altered system guided the changing forms of control provided delinquent boys.

The study will now turn to probation subsidy, a program
whose function is formally described, like that of the boys' center, as decreasing the use of state reformatories for problem
youths.

TABLE 7

REASONS FOR THE COURT INTAKE REFERRAL OF DELINQUENT
BOYS' CASES BEFORE BOYS' CENTER 1957-59

| Year | Total Offenses | Delinquent Tendencies | Specific Offenses |
|---|---|---|---|
| 1957 | 1,255 | 471 | 784 |
| % of Total Offenses | | 37.5 | 62.5 |
| 1958 | 1,576 | 560 | 1,016 |
| % of Total Offenses | | 35.5 | 64.5 |
| 1959 | 1,773 | 689 | 1,084 |
| % of Total Offenses | | 38.9 | 61.1 |
| Mean | | 573 | 961 |
| Mean Percentage | | 37.3 | 62.7 |

TABLE 8

REASONS FOR THE COURT INTAKE REFERRAL OF DELINQUENT
BOYS' CASES AFTER BOYS' CENTER 1960-62

| Year | Total Offenses | Delinquent Tendencies | Specific Offenses |
|---|---|---|---|
| 1960 | 1,743 | 608 | 1,135 |
| % of Total Offenses | | 34.9 | 65.1 |
| 1961 | 1,916 | 797 | 1,119 |
| % of Total Offenses | | 41.6 | 58.4 |
| 1962 | 1,846 | 786 | 1,060 |
| % of Total Offenses | | 42.6 | 57.4 |
| Mean | | 730 | 1,090 |
| Mean Percentage | | 39.7 | 60.3 |

FOOTNOTES--CHAPTER 3

[1]Interview with County Director of Juvenile Institutions.

[2]Albert Deutsch, Our Rejected Children (1947), pp. 118-119.

[3]The multiple functions were to insure presence in court, impress the child with the seriousness of his conduct, allow quieting down, administer punishment, etc.

[4]Governor's Special Study Commission on Juvenile Justice, Report, (1960), p. 72.

[5]Lemert, Social Action and Legal Change, p. 93.

[6]See Appendix for a description of the interview tactics and other research methods employed in this study.

[7]The data for Tables 1 through 14 are drawn from the juvenile court's Annual Probation Reports of the county Probation Officer (1967-72) and monthly intake and client flow information on file in the county's Probation Administration offices. Additional data are drawn from the yearly (1967-72) Delinquency and Probation in California Statistical Summaries for the California Youth Authority by the Bureau of Criminal Statistics: State of California.

[8]T. L. Pezman, "Untwisting the Twisted," in Probation Camps in California (Published by Camps, Ranches, and Schools Division, California Probation, Parole and Correctional Association, July, 1963), pp. 1-2.

[9]Roley Vaughn, "A Century of County Camps," California Youth Authority Quarterly, Vol. 17, No. 3 (Fall, 1964), pp. 26-31.

[10]For further information of the growth of County Treatment Institutions for youth in California see Board of Corrections, Institutions: Correctional Systems Study (State of California, Sacramento, 1971), pp. 7-15.

[11]Robert L. Smith is currently Assistant Director of Research and Development for the Youth Authority and was connected with Youth Authority research during the 1957 Camps, Ranch, and School Subsidy period. Robert Craft is currently Assistant Deputy Director of the Youth Authority's Division of Community Services. He was affiliated with Youth Authority administration during 1957.

[12]For general discussion of statistical surveys in Sociology see Aaron V. Cicourel, Measurement in Sociology (1964), pp. 14-24.

[13]For an empirical study that is based on the labeling con-

ceptualization see Aaron V. Cicourel and J. I, Kitsuse, <u>The Educa-</u>
<u>tional Decision-Makers</u> (1963), pp. 3-33.

CHAPTER 4

PROBATION SUBSIDY:   AN INTENSIVE HOME SUPERVISION
ALTERNATIVE TO STATE REFORMATORIES

In investigating the boys' center, the county juvenile court
and probation department emerged as an organization responsive
to changes that facilitated organization maintenance and expansion
rather than to changes centered on client needs.   The California
probation subsidy program was designed specifically to appeal to
these organization-oriented characteristics of county juvenile
court and probation, encouraging them to establish local alternatives to state reformatory commitments.   The appeal to organization interest was through a financial incentive program whereby
counties were encouraged to reduce their rates of commitment to
state reformatories in exchange for monetary allotments from the
state.

This chapter examines state and county involvement in probation subsidy.   An issue to be explored is the extent to which
participation in probation subsidy was dictated by perceived client treatment needs or organization interests.   Included in the
chapter will be discussion of the basis for state and county interest in probation subsidy, description of the Probation Subsidy
Act, discussion of the local perception of and subsequent adaptation to the probation subsidy program, description of the county's
operation of probation subsidy's intensive home supervision units,
and assessment of probation subsidy's impact on the form of control administered to youths by the court.

Growth Crisis in the State Youth Authority's
Correctional System

California's county juvenile court and probation practices,
before the Youth Authority's success with county subsidization,
involved differential local interpretation and adaptation of state
laws to fit perceived local needs.   As suggested in Chapter 2,
county juvenile courts and probation departments had neither clear
legal directives nor a corresponding knowledge and financial base.
Therefore, juvenile court and probation practices evolved in response to various local needs.   The Youth Authority, similar to
the Board of Charities and Corrections and the Department of Welfare, was responsible for determining state probation standards
that, by law, were voluntary.   The voluntary nature of county compliance to state probation standards led the Youth Authority to
develop a Division of Field Services comprising several consultants who provided technical advice, staff training, and practical assistance to counties in upgrading probation practices.   How-

ever, through experience the Youth Authority came to realize that --in addition to consultive services and the older techniques of statewide conferences, distribution of probation related publications, and research--other approaches were needed to overcome the strong local determination that resulted in varieties of court and probation practices.

From the Youth Authority's experimentation with techniques to lead counties in particular programmatic directions, subsidy first emerged in the 1945 Camp, Ranch, and School Subsidy Act. In 1957 the 1945 subsidy was revised to include additional state funds for counties to develop local institutions. This revision proved to be a major success, with the number of local institutions doubling within several years (see Table 3, page 36). Nonetheless, between 1950 and 1963, the Youth Authority's reformatories experienced rapid expansion because of increasing county court commitments. In 1964 it was predicted that by 1975 both the Youth Authority and the adult Department of Corrections would experience a 100 percent increase in the number of new admissions, excluding recidivists. Smith indicated this expansion problem would occur because the state had "no control over its own correctional intake, hence workloads and expenditures. State correctional workloads were directly affected by the extent to which county probation was used as an alternative for those offenders who might otherwise be committed to a state correctional agency."[1]

Since state correctional workloads were influenced by each county, it was felt necessary that the state encourage counties to reduce their rates of state commitment, thereby checking state expansion. The Youth Authority had experienced the greatest success at influencing local courts and probation services with the 1957 revision of the Camp, Ranch, and School Subsidy Act. However, Smith indicates, "the state had not declared a social policy that accepted or publicly acknowledged the reciprocal relationship between county decisions to treat or not treat locally and the consequences of that decision at the state level."[2] Furthermore, counties were not willing to give up any of their historically guaranteed rights of home rule over local services despite the problems associated with financing the operation of various court services. The importance of this strong "localism" sentiment and its restrictive role in county and state attempts to reach agreement on probation issues is summarized by Smith:

> . . . county and state efforts to reach agreement about ways to improve the probation service and standards of performance had snagged over the issue of county independence. The fork of the dilemma faced by the state was the development of standards for county probation that built in some uniformity of practice without emasculating the county's right and responsibility for local decision and action. The other fork of the dilemma pointed directly at county probation departments who recognized the need for improvements in quality and quantity of probation services but also recog-

nized that this implied the acceptance of new standards associated with any financial assistance offered by the state.[3]

Smith has identified the conflict facing local probation
administrators. They naturally wanted to take advantage of financial opportunities, but to do so they had to forsake some local
autonomy by incorporating state probation programs that might be
contradictory to local desires. Therefore, the benefits of any
state-sponsored program had to be significant for the counties to
disregard the localism issue.

## Solution to the State's Correctional Explosion: Local Intensive Home Supervision

The Youth Authority initiated research in 1961 to document
empirically the rehabilitative usefulness of less expensive community treatment programs as alternatives to state reformatories.
Phase I of this "Community Treatment Project" involved a comparative study of the consequences of reformatories and those of intensive community-based home supervision programs. Selected sub-
groups of one geographical area's delinquent population were
studied. Marguerite Warren, a project researcher, describes the
experiment as follows:

> The intake cases are first identified as eligi-
> ble or ineligible for the community based program.
> Approximately ninety percent of girls and seventy
> percent of boys have been declared as eligible, with
> the primary reason for exclusion being assaultive
> behavior. Eligible cases are then randomly assigned
> to institutional and community programs. The research
> design calls for following both those cases assigned
> to the traditional Youth Authority program (the Con-
> trols) and those cases assigned to the community pro-
> gram (the Experimentals), in terms of subsequent be-
> havior in the community and in terms of personal and
> attitude change as reflected in psychological tests
> given before and after intensive treatment.[4]

After seven years, research findings indicated that in comparing total experimental and total control cases there was "a
considerable advantage to the community-based program for all delinquent sub-types combined as indicated both in parole criteria
and in test-score changes."[5]

However, while these findings indicated higher "rehabilitative" success for the large intensive community treatment programs,
they did not identify which specific program approach or combina-
tion accounted for the increased success. Nonetheless, Warren
pointed out, "the feasibility of treating a large proportion of
the juvenile offender population in intensive community programs,
rather than institutions, was a settled issue."[6]

Following the Phase I, four substudies were carried out to specify further the desirability of community treatment compared to state institutionalization. From these studies' findings, the state claimed that at least twenty-five percent of the new admissions to the Department of Corrections and the Youth Authority in 1964 could have been retained safely locally with good home supervision. The information gathered in these four studies added to findings in a study of California probation by George Davis titled, "A Study of Adult Probation Violation Rates by Means of the Cohort Approach." Similar to the four studies, Davis concluded that California counties did not make adequate use of home supervision for many offenders.[7]

The concept emerging at the state level was that community supervision was a feasible alternative to the state's institutionally-based methods. Robert Smith states, "while the community-treatment data was irrelevant and inconclusive since it did not specify the particular community-treatment method that would yield greater rehabilitative results, it did provide a potential solution to the state's expansion crisis in corrections." The state's problem was deciding how to persuade the counties to go along with this new correctional orientation. The state had experienced success with county subsidization of juvenile institutions. Therefore, it was not surprising that the subsidy method emerged in connection with the community supervision idea. The subsidy proposals for county commitment reduction (probation subsidy) included complete state subsidization of all court services, state contracting for special probation services from the counties, a salary subsidy to enable counties to increase probation staff and decrease caseloads, postcommitment subsidy in which selected cases committed to the state would be returned to the courts and placed on probation, and a final subsidy based on county performance in reducing state commitments and developing intensive home supervision programs. Description of development and inclusion of the latter idea into the probation subsidy program and the subsequent quest for county consensus on the program follows.

## Probation Subsidy and the State Quest for Local Compliance

Formulation of the probation subsidy program began in 1964 with establishment of a state planning committee. This group was responsible for developing the intensive community supervision idea into an understandable program that would appeal to a broad range of organization interests. This planning group included Paul Mueller, who had been involved in the research studies concerning the feasibility of intensive home supervision instead of institutionalization; George Saleeby, Chief of the Youth Authority's Division of Delinquency Prevention; Walter Barkdull, Executive Officer for the Board of Corrections; Norman Rude, Sacramento State College statistician; Robert Smith and Mrs. Braithwaite, both from the Youth Authority's Research and Development Division.[8] During their first meeting, Richard McGee, Administrator of the State Youth and Adult Correction Agency, informed the group that because 1964 was a budget year rather than a policy year in the California legislature, the legislature would consider only a program that did not involve an increase in the state budget. Therefore, the group needed a program that clearly demonstrated no increase in state expenditures. Robert Smith recalled that George Saleeby had stated "if what we want to do is to keep people out of the state system, why not pay counties not to commit them?" Walter Barkdull responded with a question concerning how the state was to determine such payment for the counties in an equitable fashion.

Following the initial meeting, Smith and Braithwaite worked on developing a financial formula for the Youth Authority's cost of institutionalizing and providing successful parole services for committed youths. Smith stated they were concerned with developing a "rock bottom state career cost" that would provide base figures from which the state's county reimbursement could be derived. The assumption was that county probation departments could work with five to six persons for the same amount the state would spend on one because the counties would not rely on institutionalization. Norman Rude worked out the ultimate formula, which involved correlating three variables: (1) the state's goal of a twenty-five percent reduction of the counties' commitment of youth and adults, (2) the county average rate of commitment of offenders to the state per 100,000 population during the past five years, and (3) the dollar amount granted to counties for decreases in their base commitment rate. Counties were to receive from $2,080 to $4,000 per case depending on the percent of decrease between the base commitment rate and current commitment rates.

Once the formula was determined, the proposed program was presented to Youth Authority personnel and county probation officers. Following this step, the Youth Authority advanced the probation subsidy plan before appropriate state and county organizations before submitting the bill to the legislature.

The Probation Officer's Association was divided on the bill and, therefore, a weekend meeting between Youth Authority personnel and county probation officers was held in an attempt to increase probation officer support for the program. There was a great deal of debate about the conflict between county autonomy and the state's power to direct the ways in which counties could use their probation subsidy earnings until Lorenzo Buckley, a probation officer, stated, "since the bill was going to fly in the legislature, he would support it and they (Youth Authority and county probation departments) could work out the flaws later." Following Buckley's statement, the officers gave a vote of support for the bill and agreed to support the program with reservations.[9]

The Youth Authority's subsequent approach in promoting probation subsidy included contacts with state legislators, county judges, county boards of supervisors, etc. Initially the primary message was the potential financial gain for both the state and the counties. Further contacts were made with such interest groups as the California Congress of Parents and Teachers Associations, Federation of Women's Clubs, California Taxpayer's Associations, Juvenile Officers' Associations, National Council on Crime and Delinquency, and other fraternal and social service organizations. Support of these organizations was sought for both the probation subsidy legislation and later for implementing the program in individual counties. The Youth Authority was in a strong bargaining position even though the agencies with which it was dealing represented a variety of organization concerns. Supportive arguments for probation subsidy included its cost effectiveness, fiscal soundness, and humanitarian and rehabilitation basis.

Promotion of probation subsidy began with training selected Youth Authority personnel to deliver lectures and slide presentations designed for simple explanation of program benefits. Smith writes:

> Because of the complexity of the legislation,
> some means had to be found to present this new sub-
> sidy concept clearly and intelligently to the Gover-
> nor, State Legislators, the State Supervisors Asso-
> ciation, private citizen groups, correctional organi-
> zations and associations, boards of supervisors,
> panels of judges, and probation officers themselves.
> Initially, the public information and educational
> program conducted by the Youth Authority designed
> to sell the subsidy program, utilized conventional
> charts and graphs. These were found to be impracti-
> cal for large groups, and a better means had to be
> devised. At the encouragement of the Youth Authori-
> ty's artist, slides or transparencies for an overhead
> portable projector were developed. With the assist-
> ance of Youth Authority staff, slides were constructed
> dealing with the various aspects of subsidy. All
> verbal and graphic presentations were designed to make
> a simple and clear presentation of the proposal to
> groups representing various levels of sophistication
> and knowledge about the correctional process and the
> needs of a good probation service. Aside from promot-
> ing support, this educational campaign was also de-
> signed to neutralize potential opposition before it
> arose. As a result, organizations that might have
> opposed the subsidy plan were the first to be con-
> tacted and informed about the proposal being advanced
> by the State Board of Corrections.[10]

In summary, the probation subsidy program was supported by county government and probation staff, as well as state legislative bodies because it was interpreted as a vehicle for financial gain. Through participation, counties could receive substantial state funds that could be used to offset their increasing budgets. State reimbursement to counties, on the other hand, did not take place until after commitments were reduced and intensive home supervision services were being provided. The exchange agreements between the state and county were based on county performance with probation subsidy legislation clearly stipulating the medium of exchange as including both commitment rate reduction and corresponding operation of local intensive home supervision services. The following section describes the probation subsidy legislation.

## Probation Subsidy Legislation

The final probation subsidy program was the result of (1) a perceived state expansion crisis in both youth and adult correction institutions, (2) the state's development of an alternate plan to state institutionalization that was appealing to a range of state and county organization interests, and (3) a successful campaign by the Youth Authority that resulted in the necessary state and county consensus to implement the new program. The specific legislation for probation subsidy was divided into seven sections.[11] The sections stipulated the legislation's intent (Section 1820), the state sharing of cost (Section 1821), establishment of minimum standards by the Youth Authority (Section 1822), stipulation that the county and Youth Authority would cooperatively develop standards and procedures for probation subsidy units (Section 1823), county application for funds (Section 1824), approval of application and determination of fund reimbursement [Section 1825, (a) through (i)], and the Youth Authority's periodic reports to the legislature on subsidy program experiences and results (Section 1826).

The primary area of controversy in the probation subsidy legislation was with the Youth Authority's role in approval of county applications for state funds, calculation of commitment rate reduction, and financial reimbursement (all of which fall under Section 1824). The legislation clearly indicates that counties will not be entitled to probation subsidy funds unless the minimum subsidy standards are met. Section 1825, Subsection (a), indicates:

> No county shall be entitled to receive any state funds provided by this article until its application is approved and unless and until the minimum standards prescribed by the Department of Youth Authority are complied with and then only on such terms as are set forth hereafter in this section.

Subsections (b), (c), and (d) of Section 1825 are concerned with calculation of case commitment, annual commitment rate, and reimbursement for commitment rate reduction. Subsection (e) prescribes the method of reimbursement as follows:

> The state will reimburse the county upon presentation of a valid claim based on actual performance in reducing the commitment rate from its base rates. Whenever a claim made by a county, pursuant to this article, covering a prior fiscal year is found to be in error, adjustment may be made on a current claim without the necessity of applying the adjustment to the allocation for the prior year.

Subsection (f) stipulates that if the amount computed under Subsection (d) is less than the maximum, the difference can be used the following fiscal year.  This provision enabled counties to count on unused funds for future programs.  Subsection (g) further indicates:

> In the event a participating county earns less than the sum paid in the previous year because of extremely unusual circumstances claimed by the county and verified by the Director of the Youth Authority, with the approval of the Director of Finance, the Director of the Youth Authority may pay to the county a sum equal to the prior year's payment provided, however, that in subsequent years the county will be paid only the amount earned.

Subsection (1) clearly specifies that Probation Subsidy funds cannot be used to support existing county probation programs or to expand local institutions for youth.  Subsidy funds were to be used to develop intensive home supervision services for those youth who would have been committed to state reformatories without the availability of these services.

Subsections (f) and (g) are amendments to the original probation subsidy legislation and represent specific compromises between the state and counties.  The counties were interested in gaining state finances without state control over how the funds were used.  Yet, the way the legislation was initially written, if a county operated intensive unit programs at a cost less than their earnings, the remaining earnings had to be returned to the state.  An emergency change was made in Subsection (f) of the probation subsidy legislation to guarantee the county its surplus earnings up to one year, if the county's intensive supervision program continued to operate at a level equal to that represented by the reserved funds.  Subsection (g) was another extended financial provision for counties.  In cases where circumstances resulted in increased state commitments, the level of intensive programming could continue at the previous year's level.  This provision could be used only once with no other state reimbursements being made without state commitment reduction earnings.

Under Subsection (h) the state was able to insure particular county use of probation subsidy funds.  State law prohibits subsidies being paid twice for the same county probation service and the addition of Subsection (h) stipulated, as earlier mentioned, that probation subsidy earnings could not be spent on expansion or development of local institutions.  The state was not opposed to county expansion of local institutions, but it did not want to be involved in a double subsidy practice whereby counties would receive money for reduced commitments and, in turn, place the same youths in an institution whose construction and operation costs were financed substantially under the California's camp, ranch, and school subsidy.  In this same regard, under Section 1824 counties were required to submit to the Youth Authority their plans for intensive home supervision units.  The Youth Authority was to review the proposal to insure compliance with probation subsidy program standards before home operation initiated.  Section 1824 also provides for Youth Authority audit of extensive home supervision programs during their operation.

A major county criticism of probation subsidy was over the specification that county subsidy earnings must be used only for intensive home supervision units.  Nonetheless, even with probation subsidy's spending specifications the counties managed to juggle their subsidy spending to facilitate a variety of probation expansions that were not limited to intensive home supervision units.  Smith points out that, through "funding manipulation," some probation departments have used their probation subsidy to offset the cost of their normal growth.  In some instances, according to Smith, the subsidy earnings have encouraged counties to make excessive expenditures to take full advantage of their earnings.  In effect, counties would let their subsidy earnings dictate expansions.

## Local Perception of Probation Subsidy

The chapter will now turn to the county under study and its perception and implementation of probation subsidy.

The probation officer of the county under study initially opposed the probation subsidy bill.  As he states, "I didn't like the bill.  First, the way it was originally drawn up, you had to commit county funds to begin intensive home supervision programs before you were able to receive reduction earnings; and second, you had to spend these earnings each year."  With these specific objections in mind, this county's probation officer successfully led several probation officers in negotiating with Youth Authority probation subsidy personnel and the Youth Authority's director, Stark, to amend the legislation so counties could receive quarterly reimbursements to finance intensive supervision units.  If their earnings exceeded their expenditures, the state would hold the difference in reserve for up to one year.

To begin adapting the county's court services toward participation in the probation subsidy program, the probation officer presented his general views and specific probation subsidy strategies to the county's Superior Court Judges Committee.  The probation officer recalled, "it was not a case where I went before the judges and said we should stop committing to state institutions so we can earn $4,000 per case.  My argument was that our state commitment rates of adults and juveniles had generally been too high and now that this state money was available we could gain financing that would help us expand our local home supervision programs and lower our caseloads."

The county's strategy of program implementation was cautious.  Only one small program would be developed during the first year.  Subsequent program developments would be dictated by the county's subsidy earnings.  The probation officer explained this gradual implementation resulted from his status as a county official. "My concern was with going into the program and coming out okay financially." After the meeting with the Superior Court Judges, the probation officer arranged an information meeting about the probation subsidy program. The meeting was conducted by Robert Smith of the Youth Authority. Those invited included the juvenile court judges, members of the County Juvenile Justice Commission, and selected county probation personnel. Following this general orientation meeting, the probation officer arranged what turned out to be an all-day debate between Smith and the county auditor, who was concerned with potential county costs that could accompany county participation in the subsidy program.

Final decision for the county's participation in probation subsidy had to be made by the County Board of Supervisors. The supervisors were generally disillusioned with state or federal programs that initiated new local services. The probation officer stated local officials always were concerned that, while outside funds could help start programs, they could also be withdrawn, resulting in either increased county expenditures for continued operation or a cutback in programs. Therefore, if the county was to participate in the program, the Board of Supervisors wanted assurance that the subsidy additions (intensive home supervision units) would not require county funds. The county administrator suggested to the Board of Supervisors that it should request from the county counsel a legal interpretation of the Probation Subsidy Act.

The probation officer presented a gradual implementation plan for intensive home supervision units in which the county's financial risk was low. A conservative estimate of county subsidy earnings for reduced commitments in 1966-1967 was several times the $66,144 figure for the planned intensive home supervision unit costs. The county transferred one supervisor and three deputy probation officers into the special unit and did not hire new deputy probation officers. This meant the Board of Supervisors would not be required to increase the probation department's budget. Therefore, with this cautious probation subsidy participation plan and a county counsel interpretation that agreed with the county probation officer's interpretation of the subsidy program, the Board of Supervisors approved the plan to transfer four current probation officers into a special supervision unit. Subsequent development of additional intensive supervision units was to be determined by the county's subsidy earnings.

Chart 2 shows the county's yearly adult and juvenile state commitments, its subsidy reduction earnings, and claims against earnings for intensive programs from 1966 through 1970. The county's first year's claim for an adult unit was $67,144.09. Its earnings were $576,000 for a 144-commitment reduction from the base commitment number of 281. During the second year, 1967-1968, the county developed three additional intensive home supervision programs for juveniles with a total expenditure of $333,612.06. The first two year's expenditures totaled $400,756.15. The county lost the unclaimed balance of $175,243.85. The county's reduction

# CHART 2

## STATE PROBATION SUBSIDY – SPECIAL SUPERVISION

| | 1966-67 | 1967-68 | 1968-69 | 1969-70 (estimated) | 1970-71 (memo) |
|---|---|---|---|---|---|
| Commitment Reduction | 144 | 162 | 121 | 67 | |
| Earnings @ $4,000 per Reduction | $576,000.00 | $648,000.00 | $484,000.00 | $268,000.00 | |
| Claims Against Earnings | 67,144.09 | 333,612.06 | 569,304.25 | 484,000.00 | 268,000.00 |
| Unclaimed Earnings | -0- | 175,243.85 | 78,695.75 | -0- | -0- |
| Programs Developed | | | | | |
| Adult Unit | 67,144.09 | 125,640.06 | 141,931.14 | 117,000.00 | Tailored Programs |
| Adult Unit | | | 71,512.78 | 115,000.00 | 121,000.00 |
| Juvenile Unit | | 79,397.39 | 141,418.78 | 123,000.00 | |
| Juvenile Unit | | 100,297.14 | 168,095.16 | 126,000.00 | 142,000.00 |
| Guide – Central | | 28,277.47 | 43,878.32 | 47,000.00 | 44,000.00 |
| Adult Residence | | | 2,468.07 | -0- | |
| Total | $ 67,144.09 | $333,612.06 | $569,304.25 | $528,000.00* | $307,000.00* |

*Includes Division Director charge, diagnostic and placement costs which unless formally transferred might not be recognized as a claim against future surplus earnings – Total Approximately – $83,000.00.

earnings for 1967-1968 were $648,000.00, which was carried over for the following year's operation. In 1968-1969, the county added an adult intensive home supervision program, which brought its total number of intensive home supervision programs to five (three juvenile and two adult). Its claim for that year was $569,304.25 and earnings were $484,000.00. The county lost $78,695.75 in unclaimed earnings for the 1967-1968 period and its earnings of $484,000 were carried-over for the following year. In the 1969-1970 period the county's expenditures were $528,000, using the total carry-over figure ($484,000) with an excess of $44,000. This was transferred to the 1970-1971 expenditures for division director charges and diagnostic and placement costs. The 1970-1971 expenditures were $307,000 with earnings of only $268,000 carried over from the 1969-1970 period. The $39,000 excess was again transferred as a claim against future surplus earnings.

This substantial decrease in county earnings, because of increased commitments, immediately led the county to cut back on the intensive home supervision programs. Three of the units (two adult and one juvenile) were terminated in 1971 because of lack of funding. The county's state commitment increases in 1969-1970 were mostly juveniles. During this year the county juvenile court judge demonstrated a strong tendency to commit juveniles to state institutions, which is demonstrated in Chart 3.

In summary, the juvenile court and probation department response to reduced state commitments and substantial probation subsidy earnings was an increase in local probation services. The increase in state commitments in 1969-1970 and concurrent decrease in probation subsidy earnings resulted in a cut back of intensive home supervision programs. The level of intensive home supervision programs fluctuated with the county's financial earnings.

The county probation department claimed its expanded special supervision units had been successful in reducing recidivism among their clients. The county's 1968 Annual Probation Report states, "Two indices of the success of the Special Supervision Programs show sixty-six percent of the adult male probationers employed and twelve of those supervised by the Adult Special Programs revoked and sent to State Prison in 1968. In the juvenile units only five minors have been committed to the California Youth Authority from the intensive units over the same period."

Nonetheless, even with the stated success of the home supervision units, the department was not willing to maintain the programs without total state funding. The next section deals with operation of the county's intensive home supervision units for juveniles.

Operation of Intensive Home Supervision Units

In 1967 the county established two intensive home supervision units for juveniles. During the same year a day-care program

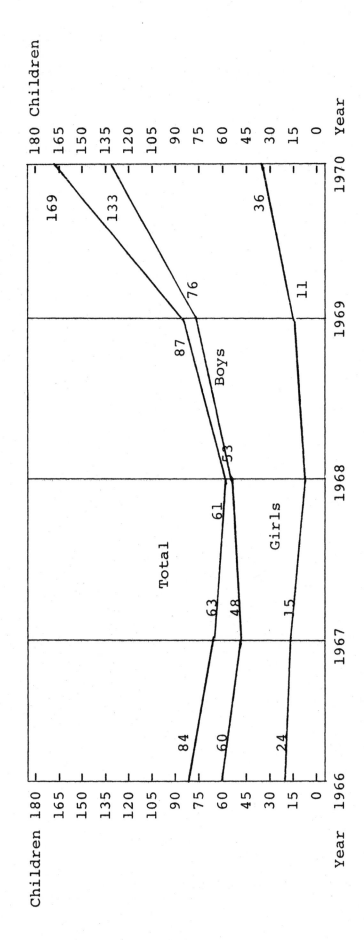

CHART 3

STATE REFORMATORY COMMITMENTS
1966 - 1970

for delinquent girls, Girls' Guide, was begun and received its funding from probation subsidy earnings. The county had developed another Girls' Guide in 1964 with Camp, Ranch, and School Subsidy funds. The two juvenile intensive home supervision units handled both boys and girls. Girls' Guide programs were for girls with particular problems in adjusting to public schools. The juvenile intensive home supervision units and Girls' Guide operated in separate facilities. Each unit handled intake of cases, program, and counseling (e.g.: group counseling, family-centered counseling, individual counseling).

The probation subsidy legislation required that all participants in intensive supervision programs must be youths who were eligible for Youth Authority commitment. Intake of cases into the county's intensive home supervision units was guided by this requirement.

The intensive home supervision caseload generally comprised youths who had problems while on regular home supervision caseloads. If a deputy probation officer with a regular caseload had a case he or she felt could be handled more suitably by intensive supervision, he or she could refer the case to the intensive unit for intake screening. The unit supervisor indicated the screening decision initially involved the unit supervisor and the unit's deputy probation officers who, as a group, would make the intake decision. The supervisor stated, "the primary requisite for admission into the unit was an expressed willingness on the part of at least one of the unit's deputy probation officers to work with the youth." Therefore, the tendency was to match a youth with a particular deputy probation officer. If this was not possible the youth was not admitted to the unit.

After a short period of operation, the intensive home supervision units found it necessary to require parental consent for participation in the intensive program before accepting a youth into the program. The county probation department stated:

> If the referral meets the guidelines set down by the state one or more intensive supervision unit deputies is assigned to read the case to determine the appropriateness of the referral, then a decision is made as to which deputy will interview the youngster and his family. The deputy referring the case may be contacted anytime during the screening process to assist in the understanding of the case. After interviewing the minor and his family a decision is made whether or not to bring the case into the unit.

> ...if the child or his family is strongly against being referred to the intensive supervision unit the chances of our successfully working with the case are nil.

In their contacts with clients, the intensive units used a variety of counseling methods, including family-centered counseling, individual counseling, group counseling, tutoring, crafts, and recreational activities. A youth receiving intensive home supervision services normally would be seen about one hour every two weeks. Parents were seen somewhat less frequently. An intensive home supervision probation officer's caseload averaged fifteen cases, which allowed them time for more frequent and longer client contacts. In a study of time spent with probationers and their families, it was determined that the intensive unit deputies spent two to three hours per month compared to what the unit supervisor claimed was fifteen minutes per month in a regular home supervision caseload.

Youths referred but not admitted to the intensive home supervision units could be referred to the boys' center, a group home, a private institution, or (in an extreme case) state reformatories. Usually some local alternative was used so the youth was not committed to the state. The intensive home supervision supervisor summarized this "something other than state reformatory" trend by stating that, "our approach was something besides the state. The Boys' Center took some of our rejects and we took some of their rejects. Once the state was knocked off as an alternative, we had to make administrative adjustments."

Therefore, there was not a direct relocation of youths who would have, without probation subsidy, gone to state reformatories. The tendency was toward local accommodation of displaced state clients. The youth who previously would have been a state reformatory client had to be redefined and placed in a different supervision category.


## Probation Subsidy Impact

The salient question to be addressed here is how the county's participation in probation subsidy influenced court related decision-making concerning troubled youths. Presumably probation subsidy should result in a displacement of clients from state reformatories into intensive home supervision. However, given the impact of the boys' center (see Chapter 3), it is not clear that these intensive home supervision programs will deal only with youths who otherwise would have been committed to the state.

Table 9 provides mean percentage comparisons of the county's youthful population, juvenile arrests, juvenile court intake referrals, and subsequent court handling three years before and three years during the operation of probation subsidy's intensive home supervision units. The proportion (mean percent) of youth population arrested decreased 1.5 percent while the proportion of youth population referred to juvenile court intake increased 1.2 percent during the first three years of probation subsidy. Referrals either closed at intake or placed under informal probation increased during 1966-1968. Additionally petitions filed for juvenile court appearance declined. The increase in referrals closed or placed under informal probation suggests either that at intake the court may have been screening youths who previously

TABLE 9

COUNTY YOUTH POPULATION, ARRESTS, JUVENILE COURT INTAKE REFERRALS
AND SUBSEQUENT DISPOSITION OF INTAKE REFERRALS

|  | Mean | |
| --- | --- | --- |
|  | 1963-65 | 1966-68 |
| Youthful Population Age 10-17 | 76,041 | 83,469 |
| Juvenile Arrests | 14,372 | 14,539 |
| Percent of Youthful Population | 18.9 | 17.4 |
| Juvenile Court Intake Referrals | 2,873 | 4,169 |
| Percent of Youthful Population | 3.8 | 5.0 |
| Referrals Closed at Intake or Placed Under Informal Probation | 1,884 | 2,886 |
| Percent of Intake Referrals | 65.6 | 69.2 |
| Petitions Filed in Juvenile Court | 989 | 1,283 |
| Percent of Intake Referrals | 34.4 | 30.8 |

would have had petitions filed or that the cases referred were
less serious in nature, which could account for fewer petitions
filed.   Summary totals of delinquent cases under some form of
court control from 1963 to 1968 are provided in Table 10.  A significant decrease in cases receiving state reformatory control occurred during the 1966-1968 period, reflecting the county's initial involvement in the probation subsidy program.   Further, an
increasing number of youths were receiving intensive home supervision services, reflective of the county's "earn and implement"
approach to probation subsidy.

Measurements of probation subsidy's impact on the extent of
state reformatory control are presented in Table 11.  Using a base
expectancy rate, an expected number of youths to receive state reformatory control was computed for the 1966-1968 period.  A comparison of the expected number with the actual number receiving
state control resulted in a decline of 55.0 percent, consistent
with the official intent of probation subsidy.  However, comparing
the estimated number of youths to be under state control, which
included the cases receiving intensive home supervision, with the
actual number, there was a 35.0 percent increase in the number of
youths controlled.  These findings indicate that probation subsidy's impact on this jurisdiction's pattern of administering control to youths extends beyond the intended displacement of cases
from the state's reformatories.  An unexpected consequence is the

TABLE 10

SUMMARY TOTALS OF DELINQUENT CASES UNDER SOME FORM OF
JUVENILE COURT OR STATE REFORMATORY CONTROL

| | 1963 | 1964 | 1965 | 1966 | 1967 | 1968 |
|---|---|---|---|---|---|---|
| Delinquent Cases Under Control | 1,254 | 1,364 | 1,408 | 1,559 | 1,637 | 1,670 |
| Delinquent Cases Receiving Some Form of Juvenile Court Control Other than Intensive Home Supervision and State Reformatory | 1,131 | 1,227 | 1,287 | 1,459 | 1,451 | 1,438 |
| Delinquent Cases Receiving Intensive Home Supervision | – | – | – | 16 | 123 | 171 |
| Delinquent Cases Receiving State Reformatory Control | 123 | 137 | 121 | 84 | 63 | 61 |
| Proportion of Delinquent Cases Under State Reformatory Control | .098 | .100 | .086 | .054 | .038 | .036 |

TABLE 11

COMPARISON OF AN EXPECTED AND AN ESTIMATED NUMBER OF DELINQUENT CASES UNDER STATE REFORMA-
TORY CONTROL IN 1966-68 WITH ACTUAL NUMBER OF DELINQUENT CASES
UNDER STATE REFORMATORY CONTROL[1]

| | | 1966-68 Mean of Actual Number of Youth Under State Reformatory Control | Difference | Percentage Change |
|---|---|---|---|---|
| Expected Number of Youth to be Under Control in the State Reformatory: | 154 | 69 | -85 | 55.0 Decrease |
| Estimated Number of Youth to be Under Control in the State Reformatory: | 51 | 69 | +18 | 35.0 Increase |

[1]To compute the expected number of delinquent youth to be subject to state reformatory control during probation subsidy's first three years of operation--a base expectancy rate is
used. The base expectancy rate is a mean of the proportion of delinquent youth under some
form of court control receiving state reformatory control during 1963-1965. The expected
number of youth to be under state reformatory control is computed by multiplying the base
expectancy rate or .095 by the mean of delinquent youth under some form of court control
during 1966-1968 or 1,622. Additionally, an estimated number of delinquent youth to be
subject to state reformatory control is provided to directly assess the impact of probation
subsidy upon the county's use of the state reformatory for delinquent youth. The estimated
number is computed by subtracting the 1966-1968 mean of delinquent youth receiving probation subsidy's intensive home supervision control (103) from the expected number of delinquent youth to be subject to state reformatory control.

inclusion of other youths previously handled by some less intensive form of court control.

In investigating the boys' center impact, it was argued that the center's operation produced a "program magnet phenomenon." To elaborate the "program magnet phenomenon" essentially involves a client displacement and new client discovery process. In terms of client displacement, new programs can, and generally are intended to, draw clients who formerly were considered suitable for a previous form of program control. Additionally, new clients previously not judged in need of program control can be judged within a less constrained framework of control alternatives, suitable for the new form of control. The intensive home supervision units were officially intended as local control alternatives for youth who, without the availability of these alternatives, would have gone to state reformatories. However, as the preceding findings demonstrate, probation subsidy's intensive home supervision control was administered to a number of youths who, in all likelihood, would not have been sent to state reformatories. Thereby, the overall control administered to the youths under court jurisdiction, increased.

A significant question that emerges from probation subsidy and boys' center impact findings concerns how these apparent liberating community-based alternatives to state reformatories result in increased control. This question will be dealt with in Chapter 6.

[1]Robert L. Smith, A Quiet Revolution:  Probation Subsidy (U. S. Department of Health Education and Welfare, DHEW Publication No. (SRS) 72-26011), p. 7.

[2]Smith, A Quiet Revolution:  Probation Subsidy, pp. 7-8.

[3]Smith, A Quiet Revolution:  Probation Subsidy, p. 10.

[4]Marguerite Warren, "The Case for Differential Treatment of Delinquents," in Harwin L. Voss (ed.), Society, Delinquency and Delinquent Behavior (1970), p. 420.

[5]Warren, "The Case of Differential Treatment of Delinquents," p. 420.

[6]Warren, "The Case of Differential Treatment of Delinquents," p. 420.

[7]George Davis, "A Study of Adult Probation Violation Rates by Means of the Cohort Approach," The Journal of Criminal Law and Criminology and Police Science (March 1964).

[8]This information was gained from interviews with Robert L. Smith.

[9]The information on this meeting was gained through interviews with the probation officer of the county under study and Robert Smith of the Youth Authority, both of whom were in attendance.

[10]Smith, "A Quiet Revolution:  Probation Subsidy," p. 29.

[11]For current legislation see California Welfare and Institutions Code, Sections 1820-1826.

CHAPTER 5


DIVERSION:  A FAMILY TREATMENT ALTERNATIVE
TO JUVENILE COURT PROCESSING


The two local court service developments previously discussed were officially aimed at moving youthful offenders out of
state reformatories and increasing the effectiveness in the treatment of young offenders.  However, examination of state and county
motives for participating in the developments suggests that a primary interest has been in the fulfillment of perceived state and
local organization needs.  In effect, the needs of youthful clients have been blurred as if organization interests and client
needs were the same.  The result of this blurring has been fluctuating patterns of court control.  Youths have been funneled into an expanding court organization structure.  An assumption reflected in this process is that expanded court services will produce more effective client treatment by the court.

This chapter examines the diversion development, which could
be interpreted as contrary to the tendency to expand the court organization (documented in Chapters 3 and 4).  Diversion is based
on the assumption that official juvenile court action may unwit-
tingly perpetuate delinquency by confirming a youth's view of him-
self as a delinquent and, thereby, facilitating further delinquency involvement.  Therefore, diversion-oriented programs attempt to "screen away" youths from the formal juvenile court system.  Officially, diversion programs are substitutes for processing of selected youths into the juvenile court system.  Consequently the inclusion of diversion services into the court system
should lead to declines in the number of clients being formally
handled.  However, while the number of formally supervised youths
would be expected to decrease, those youths who might have been
formally handled would be displaced into the new informal alternative, diversion.  As a result, without the distinction between
formal court handling and diversion, no major change should be expected in the overall number of youths receiving some form of
court-imposed control.

A primary issue to be investigated is whether the county's
incorporation of the diversion program, similar to the boys' center and the probation subsidy intensive home supervision units,
was an organization-centered development aimed at expanding the
organization components of the court or whether it was a client-
centered endeavor.

This chapter considers diversion as a federal trend, California's development of diversion into youth service bureaus,
local court adaptation to the diversion trend, the court's opera-

tion of the diversion program, and the impact of the diversion program as measured by the traditional court, and diversion control meted out to the jurisdiction's youth population.

## Diversion: A Federal Trend

In 1967 the President's Crime Commission was charged with drafting "a plan for social change responsive to the most authoritative statements concerning the problem of crime in modern America. A major purpose was to focus public attention on a balanced assessment of the weaknesses of present law and procedure."[1] One of the most widely discussed proposals of the commission was that of youth service bureaus for selected problem youths instead of juvenile court and official processing and handling.[2] The youth service bureau proposal reflected the commission's desire to narrow the juvenile court's jurisdiction and divert most troubled youths from the official juvenile court system. Specifically, the proposal reflects a recognition of the juvenile court's failure to meet its prevention, individualized treatment, and rehabilitation goals. The commission acknowledged that throughout the history of the juvenile court there has been a failure to provide the court the necessary alternatives to deal adequately with the many individual needs of the youths it served. As the commission states:

> In most places, indeed, the only alternatives are release outright, probation, and institutionalization. Probation means minimal supervision at best. A large percentage of juvenile courts have no probation services at all, and in those that do, caseloads are typically so high that counseling and supervision take the form of occasional phone calls and perfunctory visits instead of the careful, individualized service that was intended. Institutionalization too often means storage - isolation from the outside world - in an overcrowded, understaffed, high-security institution with little education, little vocational training, little counseling or job placement or other guidance upon release.[3]

However, the commission concluded the infusion of resources for expanding existing court services would not result in the court's fulfillment of its original goal of providing individualized treatment and rehabilitation for troubled youths.

In contrast to the familiar argument of inadequate resources, the commission connects the juvenile court's failure to fulfill its prevention, treatment, and rehabilitation goals to unrealistic expectations. These expectations are based on the court's "grossly over-optimistic view of what is known about the phenomenon of juvenile criminality and of what even a fully equipped juvenile court could do about it."[4] The commission maintains that juvenile corrections experts agree it is most difficult to develop methods that prevent delinquent acts through rehabilitation programs because of a lack of understanding of the delinquency phenomenon. Theories of delinquency offer varieties of general explanations. Despite the more recent attempts to narrow these explanations, the commission points out:

> Some have noted the enormous variety in the types of conduct officially denominated delinquency as well as in the types of juveniles found to be delinquents and have begun to suggest narrower explanations differentiating among kinds of deviant behavior. But fundamentally delinquency is behavior, and until the science of human behavior matures far beyond its present confines, an understanding of those kinds of behavior we call delinquency is not likely to be forthcoming. Study and research tend increasingly to support the view that delinquency is not so much an act of individual deviance as a pattern of behavior produced by a multitude of pervasive societal influences well beyond the reach of the action of any judge, probation officer, correctional counselor or psychiatrist.[5]

The juvenile court's overly optimistic view of what causes youthful criminality and what can prevent or correct it is viewed as having provided a basis for extending official control, overshadowed by the fact that much of the official action may do more harm than good. The underlying assumption is that official juvenile justice agencies such as the police, juvenile court, probation, and correction institutions create or support delinquency by focusing their attention on certain youth. The commission specifically argues:

> Official action may actually help to fix and perpetuate delinquency in the child through a process in which the individual begins to think of himself as delinquent and organizes his behavior accordingly. That process itself is further reinforced by the effect of the labeling upon the child's family, neighbors, teacher, and peers, whose reactions communicate to the child in subtle ways a kind of expectation of delinquent conduct. The undesirable consequences of official treatment are heightened in programs that rely on institutionalizing the child. The most informed and benign institutional treatment of the child, even in well designed and staffed reformatories and training schools, thus may contain within it the seeds of its own frustration and itself may often feed the very disorder it is designed to cure.[6]

Therefore, the juvenile court--in addition to lacking the knowledge, techniques, facilities, and personnel to carry out their individualized treatment and rehabilitation goals--can by its contact with a troubled youth stigmatize and thereby further his involvement in delinquency. Nonetheless, even with these criticisms of the juvenile court, the commission does not recommend a relocation of juvenile court functions or its abolishment,

but instead argues for a revision in the juvenile court's philosophy toward "more reachable goals." The commission summarizes that
the juvenile court's reach had exceeded its grasp, which led to
philosophical and operational discrepancies. As the commission
states:

> In theory the court's operations could justifia-
> bly be informal, its findings and decisions made with-
> out observing ordinary procedural safeguards, because
> it would act only in the best interest of the child.
> In fact it frequently does nothing more nor less than
> deprive a child of liberty without due process of law
> - knowing not what else to do and needing, whether ad-
> mittedly or not, to act in the community's interest
> even more imperatively than the child's. In theory it
> was to exercise its protective powers to bring an er-
> rant child back in the fold. In fact there is increas-
> ing reason to believe that its intervention reinforces
> the juvenile's unlawful impulses. In theory it was to
> concentrate on each case the best of current social
> science learning. In fact it has often become a vested
> interest in its turn, loathe to cooperate with innova-
> tive programs or avail itself of forward-looking meth-
> ods.[7]

Based on the philosophy versus operation discrepancy, the
commission argues that the juvenile court should alter its philosophy and goals so they do not "outrun reality." The commission
reasoned that the juvenile court, as a court of law, is charged
with protecting the community against threatening conduct. While
rehabilitation through individualized handling of problem youths
is one way of providing community protection, the court's jurisdiction should be narrowed down to only "those cases of manifest
danger." Further, the court should infuse procedures "to assure
fair and reliable determinations" for cases serious enough for
judicial action.[8] Problem youths who are not imminent risks to
the community but are in need of redirection, the commission argues, should be screened away from the court and receive prej-
udicial dispositions into agencies outside the formal juvenile
justice system. Such agencies could include mental health agencies, social agencies, school guidance units, family counseling,
and other community services.

The community youth service approach, as a substitute to
juvenile court handling, was to be carried out in what the commission termed "youth service bureaus." The commission recommended
that "communities should establish neighborhood youth serving
agencies, youth service bureaus, located if possible in comprehensive neighborhood community centers and receive both delinquent
and non-delinquent youth."[9] While some of the cases could be referred by parents, schools, or other sources, most referrals would
originate from the police and court intake. If after study, certain youths were determined unlikely to benefit from its services,
the bureau could notify the referral source of its decision not to
service the particular case. Primary function of the bureau was

to provide individually tailored service for youths in trouble. The commission reasoned this individual service could include "group, individual, and family counseling; placement in group or foster homes; work and recreational programs; employment counseling; and special educational services (remedial and vocational). The coordination of the youth and his family to the service agency would be under the direct control of the bureau, the key to success being the voluntary participation by the youth and his family in following the rehabilitation plan."[10]

Purpose of the youth service bureaus was three-fold: avoiding stigma, relying on more appropriate agencies for problem youth, and energizing community involvement. Margaret Rosenheim suggests these goals are very much a part of the middle-class approach to juvenile problems:

> Middle-class parents not only work to develop
> the social utilities of a Good Life (e.g., Boys Scouts,
> community centers with youth programs, good schools
> with strong supporting services) but they also invest
> their energies individually and vigorously to head off
> the risk of stigma attaching to their own precious
> children, when and if their children run afoul with
> authority. They are sensitive and quick to react to
> unlawful behavior by officials. Middle-class parents
> are also aided by their ability to tap alternatives
> to official legal intervention into the lives of
> their children. Many of them are so positioned as
> to be able to "buy a little time" at camp, to enroll
> a youngster in a remedial reading class, to arrange
> a school transfer through cajolery (sometimes even
> threat!), to send a child out-of-town to military
> academy or to Aunt Jane's for a period, or, in the
> case of pregnant daughters, to arrange discreetly
> for abortion or adoption in a distant place. But
> these alternatives are unavailing to children of the
> poor, largely because the money needed to secure them
> is unavailable.[11]

In essence, youth service bureaus emerge as a youth or family service agency delivering a variety of services in substitution for juvenile court processing.[12] Services were to be delivered to both delinquent youths and youths felt to be moving into delinquent-oriented behavior. Primary goal of the bureaus is to assist youths in solving their problems without subjecting them to the stigmatizing effects presumed associated with juvenile court contact. While the commission provided the general concept of the youth service bureau, it did not specify how the bureaus were to accomplish their tasks. The commission left the organization of the bureaus to the state or the local communities interested in establishing them.[13]

## California's Development of Diversion into Youth Service Bureaus

California's Youth Service Bureau approach reflected the President's Commission recommendation. William Underwood, in an article pertaining to California's establishment of youth service bureaus, points out that Howard Ohmart of the California Youth Authority was a staff member and contributing author on the President's Commission. Underwood writes:

> Upon returning to California, Mr. Ohmart reported the events of his eighteen months' work with the National Crime Commission. The recommendation which attracted the most interest and support related to the establishment of Youth Service Bureaus. Former Youth Authority Director, Heman Stark, a leader in the field of prevention, stimulated interest in discussion and action in behalf of developing this concept. Responsive individuals in authority who moved this concept from an idea to a reality included Senator George Deukmejian of Long Beach; Sheriff Mike Canlis, San Joaquin County; and members of the California Delinquency Prevention Commission.[14]

Robert Smith and Robert Craft of the Youth Authority indicated that Stark, after reading the President's Commission report, stated that he wanted California to be the first state to implement the youth service bureau concept. To promote support for youth service bureaus in California, Stark decided a law enforcement official should write the first article arguing for the local development of bureaus in California and their potential use by law enforcement. In 1968 Michael Canlis, the Sheriff of San Joaquin County and a member of the California Delinquency Prevention Commission, wrote such an article and indicated the urgent need for California to move ahead with the youth service bureau approach. He stated,

> We cannot continue to put off the development of a program that embodies the principles of the Youth Service Bureau. The growing problem of juvenile delinquency which California faces demands that we act now if we are to be able to handle our predictable future population.[15]

He further argued that much of what is needed to establish youth service bureaus could be accomplished within the framework of existing resources through realignment of public and private services and without an increase in funding.

Later that same year, Smith, Craft and Oldfield (an assistant to State Senator George Deukmejian), worked on writing a youth service bureau bill. Senator Deukmejian introduced the legislation, Senate Bill 892, April 5, 1968, which detailed the organization and functions of youth service bureaus. Included were state funding provisions to establish four local pilot youth service bureaus that would be required to meet the program guidelines to be established by the California Delinquency Prevention Commission. The Youth Service Bureau Act (Section 1900-1905 of the California Welfare and Institutions Code) was passed by both the Assembly and the Senate on August 1, 1968. Section 1902 stipulated that in implementing the legislation the California Delinquency Prevention Commission was to cooperate with local county Delinquency Prevention Commissions and the Youth Authority on (1) the establishment of program guidelines and (2) the selection of the four programs from locally submitted proposals. The following two paragraphs state the essential standards developed by a joint effort of the above mentioned groups:

> The purpose of the Youth Service Bureau Act is to offer an incentive and opportunity for local agencies (both public and private) to pool their resources and develop innovative programs to divert young people from entering into the juvenile justice system. The Youth Service Bureau is a place in the community to which delinquent and delinquent prone youths can be referred by parents, law enforcement agencies, the schools, etc.. It should have a wide range of services reflecting the coordination and integration of important public and private prevention resources existing in the community . . .

> A neighborhood center is envisioned in a location central to the community (or a target area within the community) with day to day operations and services under the direction of a Youth Services Coordinator. Participating agencies, organizations, and volunteers would contribute full or part-time staff and supportive services for the children and youth served.[16]

Following development of youth service bureau guidelines, information concerning the legislation and the program standards was disseminated to each of the California county Delinquency Prevention Commissions. A meeting was held in Southern California and one in Northern California to review with county delinquency commission representatives the established guidelines for youth service bureaus. During these meetings interest was stimulated for developing local proposals. In addition, the information on youth service bureaus and the availability of state funds was distributed to various community groups including chiefs of police, probation officers, sheriffs, California Council on Children and Youth, County Juvenile Justice Commissions, Urban League, NAACP, United Fund Organizations, and local community action groups (League of Women Voters, Lawyers' Wives, etc.). These groups received descriptions of the youth service bureau legislation and the deadlines regarding the submission of proposals for the four pilot youth service bureau projects.[17] Before selection of the four pilot projects, the Youth Authority applied for Law Enforcement Assistance Administration (LEAA) funds from the California Council on Criminal Justice (CCCJ) to assist in funding additional youth service bureaus. The LEAA application was approved and the state received a $150,000 federal grant to increase the number of pilot projects to nine. The remaining funds were to be used for evaluating the projects by the Youth Authority's Division of Research and Development.

In early February, 1969, the nine pilot projects were selected from a total of twenty-five proposals. The stated selection criteria were: (1) eligibility in accordance with published guidelines and standards, (2) degree of community involvement of both public and private agencies, (3) program content, (4) uniqueness of target area and connection between target area needs and youth service bureau program, (5) and a demonstration that the bureau is not a part of an existing program. State funding for these projects was discontinued in June, 1971. This action resulted in termination of the federal funds because of a grant condition requiring matching state funds. Eight of the youth service bureau pilot projects subsequently applied directly to CCCJ through a local (city or county) unit of government for refunding for the fiscal year 1971-1972. The local unit (i.e.: county probation department) provided the required matching funds, approximately 20 percent, through in-kind services. Through this method the counties were able to expand the youth service bureaus (now being termed "Special Grant Diversion Units") substantially beyond the previous $25,000 annual level.

In summary, diversion was a federal trend that included provision of state and federal funds for local programs meeting funding guidelines. Local agencies could receive funds in exchange for adopting a particular form of diversion program. Therefore, the incorporation of diversion programs by county agencies can be explained, in part, as an expected organization response to an external financial opportunity.

## Local Adaptation to the Diversion Trend

The jurisdiction under study was one of the nine counties selected for a state and federally funded youth service bureau pilot program. The county's Delinquency Prevention Commission encouraged several cities in the county to develop youth service bureau program proposals to be entered in the statewide competition. Three cities submitted proposals. The one selected was developed by what was called the "Inter-Agency Committee," which included representatives from a number of local organizations. One local organization that participated in the development of the proposal selected was the Model Cities Group. When the proposal was approved, the Delinquency Prevention Commission and Model Cities personnel worked together on the selection of a program coordinator. In addition to the program coordinator, several county agency personnel were loaned for four hours a week to the bureau. The personnel included a deputy probation officer, a police officer, an employment counselor, a psychiatrist, and a public health nurse. Two paraprofessionals worked with the bureau full-time. The bureau was in operation two years and, according to its reports, made contacts with more than 500 youths. Most of these contacts involved assistance in job placement. The youth service bureau was discontinued when the state and federal funds terminated.

The pilot program provided the basic philosophical and operational framework that the juvenile court and probation department used in its move into diversion. A perceived financial opportunity led to the county juvenile court and probation department's interest in diversion. The financial opportunity was first communicated to the probation officer by the county administrator. In the county, a city that received a substantial Model Cities grant appropriated a portion of its funds for delinquency prevention programs. The probation officer summarized, "The Model Cities concept involved the use of citizen task force groups to determine various city needs. One task force was concerned with crime reduction and decided that the prevention of delinquency was a primary need. Therefore, we (the probation department) became involved in attempting to fill this need, through the utilization of Model Cities funds." The Model Cities Agency was familiar with securing federal grants and this led to a partnership between the Model Cities Agency and the probation department. The two organizations combined efforts to develop a federal proposal through CCCJ for two county diversion programs. One program would deal with the Model Cities target area (western county) while the second extended the diversion efforts into the central area of the county.

The county's move into diversion through the securing of federal grants is explained by the county probation officer as being "a fashionable trend of the time in going after federal grants" and a "natural administrative response to available funds." The probation officer elaborated that during the late 1960's many city and county government agencies (law enforcement, employment, health, social welfare, etc.) looked for federal grants. Beginning during the Johnson administration federal funds for local social services were increasingly available. In the justice area, this trend is demonstrated by the Omnibus Crime Bill and the Safe Streets Act of 1968, which created the Law Enforcement Assistance Administration (LEAA) in the U. S. Department of Justice. LEAA required establishment of a planning agency (CCCJ in California) in each state to administer the federal bloc grant program to state or local programs meeting federal guidelines oriented toward reducing crime through the improvement of the criminal justice system. Therefore, given the large amounts of federal funds being made available for delinquency control, the county probation officer stated, "It was only natural to go after the funds that would assist us in the expansion of our court services." In this statement the probation officer reflects his view of local government as an adaptable mechanism that must be able to take advantage of opportunities that will help fulfill perceived organization maintenance and expansion needs.

In exchange for federal funds local agencies developed federally-prescribed diversion programs reflecting particular programmatic priorities in favor at the time. Shortly after the

President's Commission report on crime and delinquency and congressional appropriation of funds (through the Safe Streets Act), diversion became "the name of the game for federal funding," according to the director of the county diversion program. As more federal money became available, CCCJ began to give greater priority to proposals submitted by law enforcement, court, and correctional agencies that included diversion program orientations. The favoring of traditional agencies over alternate ones (i.e.: private agencies) was because the formal agencies became more adept at submitting successful grant proposals and the funding procedures became more institutionalized. This is clearly the case currently with the reorganization of CCCJ into what is termed the "regional systems approach." With this approach, each regional CCCJ agency determines its goals and funding priorities within the general state framework and distributes its bloc grant funds accordingly. Before the regional approach, all CCCJ grant proposals and decision-making were handled at the state level.

The county juvenile court and probation department's diversion program included, in addition to CCCJ grant money, HEW Model Cities funding for its youth house. Additionally, the drug abuse prevention education and training component is funded through a separate CCCJ grant to a city police department for a program of delinquency control and diversion. Chart 4 illustrates the organization components and funding resources of the county's diversion program.

CHART 4

DIVERSION PROGRAM COMPONENTS

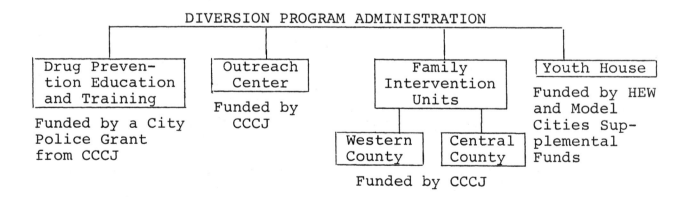

## Diversion Program Operation

The diversion program became operational in early 1972. The earlier youth service bureau had been administered jointly by the county Delinquency Prevention Commission and the Model Cities group. The change in name from youth service bureau to diversion program was an attempt by the new program director to eliminate connection between the old and new programs. This change was deemed necessary because of the belief that the earlier program had not been successful. Nonetheless, the new diversion program was modeled on the same philosophy and general goals of the earlier program, including delinquency prevention, family crisis intervention, and diversion from the formal juvenile court system. The diversion program included four interrelated program components: the drug abuse prevention education unit, the Outreach center, the family intervention units, and the neighborhood youth house.

The drug abuse prevention unit's function is primarily to educate community groups about different drugs, rehabilitation and counseling techniques for drug users, and the available community treatment resources for drug users. The drug abuse prevention unit can serve both public and private groups, but primarily deals with juvenile court, probation, and police. The unit's operations are a part of the overall attempt by the diversion program to coordinate community resources into an understandable and usable referral system for various youth related problems. The unit's focus on drug-related education and coordination of referral resources is directly related to the availability of funds for drug-related services. The police department of the city in which the diversion program's target population is primarily located received a federal grant, part of which was designated for drug-abuse prevention and treatment. The city police department, in turn, transferred the funds for drug-abuse prevention and treatment into the diversion program to provide for the salaries of a full-time program coordinator and a half-time secretary.

The unit, which became fully operational in June, 1972, established a drug-abuse referral system to which individuals in need of assistance or consultation about drug problems could be referred for help. The county juvenile court and probation department and the diversion program components used the program in cases involving youths judged to be in need of a drug-treatment referral. However, according to the diversion program director, the primary function of the drug program was to train and familiarize court and diversion staff on the handling of drug problems and the community referral resources available. Spergel has noted "community-work and direct-service organizations are aware of the importance of coordination. However, they often do not have sufficient resources to support the community."[18] The drug abuse prevention unit is oriented toward providing this service.

The outreach center component of the diversion program focuses on individual counseling and youth group work and assists other community agencies that offer youth services. The underlying assumption involved in the outreach center's activities is that delinquency is the result not only of a youth's behavior, but also of a lack of constructive involvement by community residents and organizations. The center's staff includes the diversion program director, a program developer, counseling staff (deputy probation officers), clerical workers, and a cadre of Neighborhood

Youth Corps students, volunteers, and donated staff from public agencies. Spergel refers to this community work approach to delinquency as the "developer role." He states:

> The developer in the low-income area sees the delinquent as having limited access to economic and social opportunities and all slum dwellers as having no participation in the culture and activities of the larger society. But these are not critical determinants of the delinquency problem. The developer believes also that the culture of the slum may have many positives. The slum may provide a fairly adequate, if minimal, system of rewards for its members. Further, it can be made a decent place in which to live and grow up. The problem is to maximize potentials of the people to make the most of the situation.[19]

Spergel's description of the "developer" community worker corresponds with the way the outreach center approached services, which are separated on the basis of direct and indirect services. The direct services include such activities as individual or group counseling, employment assistance, tutoring services, and what the center terms "cultural enrichment experiences." In addition, the outreach center sponsors youth clubs, athletic teams, karate classes, sewing classes, and youth leadership training conferences. The outreach center facility also serves as a drop-in center for youths to shoot pool, play quiet games, or engage in rap sessions. These activities are stated to be used in a therapeutic manner. "They are developed in an effort to help the youngster develop a positive self-image and greater interest in relating to others."

Indirect services provided to the general community include assisting other agencies in developing youth programs. These agencies include the Economic Opportunity Youth Council, a Neighborhood House, the Southside Center Youth Program, and a neighborhood referral center for the diversion program. The diversion program director stated the outreach center serves the community both in an advisory capacity for youth-oriented problems and neighborhood youth projects (e.g.: neighborhood house--a drop-in center) and as a central coordinating agency that can assist community groups in gaining access to various economic, educational, and advisory resources for youth related services.

The outreach center's direct program contact with youths begins with either an agency, parental, or self referral. Self referrals usually are by youths seeking employment assistance that can either result in a direct referral to a local employment agency or, in many instances, an interview conducted in an attempt to assist the youth in what one of the counselors stated as a realistic job orientation (e.g.: what are you qualified for?). In these instances further education or specific job training could be recommended. According to one deputy probation officer in the outreach center, many of the self referrals originate from the police informally. In these cases the police may make a follow-up to verify contact. The regular law enforcement referral is made through a citation system. The police issue a citation to the youth and send a copy to the outreach center. After receiving the citation, the outreach center makes three attempts to contact the youth--first by telephone, then by letter and finally by a visit to the youth's home. Following the center's contact and screening, a disposition is reached that can include individual counseling, involvement in center activities, or referral to the diversion program's family intervention units for family counseling. The most frequent disposition is individual counseling with a regular caseworker. Verification of the center's contact and disposition is then forwarded to the police. Generally, a youth's contact with the center should not exceed six months, although many cases have extended beyond this period. The diversion program director stated he has begun to require written statements by the caseworkers explaining why a case should be continued beyond six months.

The youth house component of the diversion program is used as an alternative to the county detention facility or shelter for selected youths, aged thirteen to eighteen. The youth house can accommodate up to eight girls and boys. Their stay is not to exceed four months. The house staff consists of a full-time director, half-time secretary, and two houseparents. Youth house residents are referred by themselves, their parents, other diversion units, juvenile court intake, or police. In most instances the house provides temporary residence for youths whose parents will not allow them to return home at the time or youths who are likely to experience further problems if immediately returned home. Once a minimal level of reconciliation between the youth and the parents is achieved, the youth is returned home and the family normally begins the family counseling offered in the family intervention units. If reconciliation is not achieved, a petition is filed in the juvenile court and a suitable out-of-home placement is sought.

The family intervention units are the most direct diversion units in the program because they serve as a specific alternative to juvenile court processing of cases, usually at the juvenile court intake stage. In contrast, the outreach center is aimed at developing youths in the community to prevent delinquency or other youth problems. The family intervention units receive primarily incorrigible cases, youth whose problems are viewed as family centered. A county-prepared description of the family intervention units specifies the cases that can be handled by the units:

1.  Only cases whose parents or guardians reside in the target city limits.

2.  All 601 cases admitted to the juvenile hall that are presently not active.

3.  All citations for 601's (these cases can involve a minor 602 offense or truancy if it is determined to be incidental to the 601 aspect of the

84

case).

4. Minor 602 cases (i.e.: petty theft, malicious mischief, curfew, alcoholic offenses (non-traffic), drug cases (involving possession or use but not selling), burglary by a youth 14 years or younger, joyriding and other misdemeanors) admitted to the juvenile hall that are not presently active or have been dismissed 90 days or longer.

5. No cases of great public notoriety will be handled by the projects.

6. Offenses which will not be included in the project are selling drugs, robbery, burglary by a 15 year old or above, grand theft auto, traffic offense, and offenses involving violence or sexual assault.

The intervention units offer family counseling services to youths and their families in cases where a youth's incorrigibility, truancy, runaway, or other miscellaneous behavior problems are determined to be as a result of a family-centered problem. The guiding assumption is that a youth's behavior problems are "relative and proportionate to the transaction and communication among family members and cannot be helped without family participation."[20]

The family intervention process generally begins with a family crisis situation in which the youth is separated from the family (i.e.: juvenile court intake) or nearing the point where the parents are considering having the youth removed from the home. The casework supervisor of one unit explained that in most instances the parents have the youth placed in detention for punishment and as an indication that if the child does not meet their behavior expectations in the future they will take formal action. The supervisor contends that in the case of many minority families, while they attempt to punish the youth by turning him over to the police and juvenile court, they feel guilty about "turning the kid over to the man." In these instances the parents are interested in getting the youth back home with the thought that now the child knows they will take formal action. Therefore, to get the youth home these families will generally agree to family intervention's minimum of five counseling sessions in which both the youth, the parents, and the siblings must be present. In cases involving non-minority families, the casework supervisor and the diversion program director contended that financial coercion was a common tactic in convincing the parents to participate in the family intervention program. The general argument put forth by family-intervention staff is that if the youth remains in juvenile hall, a petition will be filed and after several days stay at the hall the youth will likely be returned home anyway. The result will be a billing of the parents for the youth's stay in detention. In addition, the casework supervisor continued, "We include alot of propaganda as to the negative effects a stay in detention can have on a youth." It should be pointed out that in the period before diversion's family intervention operation, a youth's first referral to detention intake on a 601 or minor 602 offense normally would result in the intake officer contacting the youth's parents to arrange a release outright or a release on informal probation without supervision. For example, a comparison of 1971 and 1972, diversion's first year, one unit's detention intake shows that of 296 referral cases, 195 (40 percent) were closed at intake while in 1972 of a 266 total referral cases only 10 (4 percent) were closed at intake. This is why the county's probation officer stated, "we felt 'diversion' to be a way of implementing good informal probation."

The five family intervention counseling sessions begin with a caseworker's attempt to observe what is going on in the family unit and then to offer remedies for the family's problems. The intervention counselor attempts to diagnose the problems and bring them out into the open. Once there is an acknowledgment of the problem a more permanent form of therapy is sought through various referral sources. One of the most frequently used referrals by the family intervention units is that of probation. According to the casework supervisor those youth referred to probation from the family intervention units usually receive an out-of-home placement, a foster home or an institution. This suggests that in those instances where a youth is not able to comply with the diversion program requirements the youth generally is considered inappropriate for the probation department's regular home supervision. Other referral sources include County Mental Health; County Social Service; Home, Health, and Counseling Service (a local agency), the probation department's family service worker; and marital counseling groups. The casework supervisor stated that in all cases involving other agency referrals the caseworker is required to accompany the family as a group or individual members to the first several counseling sessions. Following this the caseworker maintains contact with the referral source to monitor the progress of the family or individual members.

In summary, the county's diversion program components and their operation are based on the assumption that through the coordination of community resources the problem of delinquency can be overcome. Overall delinquency is viewed as primarily the result of what Lemert terms a "dilapidated social structure," which produces not only troubled individuals but multiproblem families as well.[21] As evidenced in the description of the operation of the diversion program components, the distinction between individual youths and their families is not sharply maintained. However, while many writers in the field of delinquency connect the family with delinquent conduct, the connection is based on a statistical, not causal relationship, which does not separate the influence of the family from other intervening variables such as poverty, slum residence, and lack of education. Nonetheless, and despite the lack of an empirical justification for family intervention, the county's units are expanding with current proposed program additions to be directed at what the diversion program director terms "earlier and earlier intervention" into families that are beginning to experience problems with their children.

The concept of diversion is predicated on the assumption that the formal juvenile court system is destructive and that it is more effective to direct problem youths to a program that is less stigmatizing than to escalate him through the formal justice system.

However, the issue that emerges is that diversion in practice is an extension of the court's control over youths and their families. Diversion's family-intervention thrust toward earlier detection of families with problem youths, therefore, appears to conflict with the recommended restricted jurisdiction nation underlying the diversion concept.

## Diversion Program Impact

In Table 12, arrest and court handling comparisons are made between the 1972 percentages and the mean percentages for 1969 to 1971. These comparisons appear consistent with the official goal of diversion as expressed by the President's Commission: to divert youth away from the formal juvenile court process. The 1972 arrests, juvenile court intake referrals, and cases receiving juvenile court petitions each indicate percentage declines from the 1969 to 1971 mean percentages. These declines are likely related to diversion's operation. In 1972 the police were able to refer selected youths to diversion instead of arresting and referring to juvenile court intake. Fewer arrests and court intake referrals, together with more cases closed at intake or placed under informal probation, account for the decreased number of juvenile court petitions. Availability of diversion provides probation intake staff with an alternative to traditional juvenile court processing and results in fewer juvenile court petitions filed.

During 1972 the diversion units received a total of 1,691 referrals. The referrals originated from probation, police, parents, schools, and self. Only nine of the total 1,691 referrals were closed at intake. Of the 1,682 diversion clients, 1,179 received family intervention service, 54 resided at the youth house, and 449 were handled by the outreach center. The disproportionate number of youths receiving family services is attributable to the presence of a large number of indirect sibling referrals. The presence of parents and of all children in the family was required in the family intervention process.

The summary totals of youths under some form of court and diversion control from 1969 to 1972 are presented in Table 13. Included are the proportions of youth population under control. Differentiation is made between direct and indirect sibling referrals. Between 1971 and 1972 there was a numerical increase of 823 in the number of youths under some form of control and an increase of from .03 to .04 when compared to all youths in the jurisdiction. The portion of youths directly referred and under con-

TABLE 12

COUNTY YOUTH POPULATION, ARRESTS, JUVENILE COURT INTAKE REFERRALS
AND SUBSEQUENT DISPOSITION OF INTAKE REFERRALS

|  | Mean | |
| --- | --- | --- |
|  | 1969-71 | 1972 |
| Youthful Population<br>  Age 10-17 | 86,910 | 88,316 |
| Juvenile Arrests<br>  Percent of Youthful Population | 14,348<br>16.5 | 12,447<br>14.1 |
| Juvenile Court Intake Referrals<br>  Percent of Youthful Population | 5,612<br>6.5 | 4,661<br>5.3 |
| Referrals Closed at Intake or<br>  Placed Under Informal Probation<br>  Percent of Intake Referrals | 3,428<br>61.1 | 3,201<br>68.7 |
| Petitions Filed in Juvenile Court<br>  Percent of Intake Referrals | 2,184<br>38.9 | 1,460<br>31.3 |

TABLE 13

SUMMARY TOTALS OF YOUTH UNDER SOME FORM OF JUVENILE COURT OR
DIVERSION CONTROL AS A RESULT OF DIRECT COURT INTAKE
REFERRALS AND INDIRECT SIBLING REFERRALS
TO DIVERSION'S FAMILY INTERVENTION

|  | 1969 | 1970 | 1971 | 1972 |
| --- | --- | --- | --- | --- |
| Directly Referred Youth Receiving<br>  Informal, Formal, or Diversion<br>  Control | 2,755 | 2,285 | 2,676 | 2,713 |
| Indirect Sibling Referrals to<br>  Diversion's Family Intervention<br>  Control | – | – | – | 786 |
| Total Youth Under Some Form of Pro-<br>  bation or Diversion Control | 2,755 | 2,285 | 2,676 | 3,499 |
| Proportion of County Youth Popula-<br>  tion Under Control | .03 | .03 | .03 | .04 |

trol remained constant in 1972 as in the previous years, but when the indirect sibling referrals are included, the proportion increased substantially.

Table 14 provides measurement of the change in the numbers of youths under control as a result of diversion's operation. Using a base expectancy rate, an expected number of youths to be under control was computed for 1972. A comparison of the expected number with actual numbers, differentiated again on the basis of direct and indirect sibling referrals, resulted in increase from 2.4 percent to 32.1 percent. If it were available, a measure of time youths spend under control would have been useful, since the "amount of control" is a function of both the number of persons under control and the amount of time they spend under control. Additionally, since diversion's family intervention service is not limited to directly-referred youth and their siblings, but includes the parents as well, the extension of control presented here is an underestimate because the parents have not been included in the family intervention numerical totals.

Of the 1,179 youths receiving diversion's family intervention service, 88 ultimately received juvenile court petitions requesting suitable out-of-home placements. These 88 youths were referred to the juvenile court because their families were unable or unwilling to comply with the family intervention methods. It was reasoned by the family intervention units' staff that if families did not respond to the family-centered treatment, the child (and siblings) should be removed from the home. Failure to comply or to progress with family treatment was felt to indicate family disorganization. Essentially, families found not amenable to family intervention were viewed as possessing limited potential in providing the appropriate child-socialization necessary to prevent future troublesome behavior.

A significant issue that emerges from the preceding findings concerns how the larger umbrella of social control resulting from diversion relates to depressing, creating, or accelerating delinquency. This reflects, in part, the concerns that have grown out of the labeling theory literature in the last two decades. As discussed in Chapter 1, labeling theorists have argued that formal interaction with social control agencies is an important component involved in the perpetuation of delinquency.[22] While the data for the present study are not intended to address this issue, several implications emerged. Specifically, these findings have shown diversion to produce expanded control as measured by larger numbers of youth receiving some form of juvenile court service, as well as accelerated control as determined by the out-of-home placement of youths whose families are unable or unwilling to comply with family intervention. In the latter instance, what often occurs is that siblings with no prior behavior problem are accelerated into the formal court system for what is termed a "suitable out-of-home placement." Suitable out-of-home placements can include placement with relatives or in a foster home, group home, or institution. The potential of this practice to accelerate youth behavior problems or actually to create delinquency warrants serious research consideration.[23]

TABLE 14

COMPARISON OF THE EXPECTED NUMBER OF YOUTH UNDER CONTROL
IN 1972 WITH ACTUAL NUMBER OF YOUTH UNDER CONTROL
INCLUDING A TWO SIBLING ESTIMATE[1]

|  | Expected Number of Youth to be Under Control | Difference | Percentage Increase |
|---|---|---|---|
| Actual Number of Youth Under Control: | 2,713 2,649 | +64 | 2.4 |
| Actual Number of Youth Under Control Including a Two Sibling Estimate: | 3,499 2,649 | +850 | 32.1 |

[1]To compute the expected number of youth to be under some form of control during diversion's first year of operation--a base expectancy rate is used. The base expectancy rate is a mean of the proportion of county youth population under control during 1969-1971. The expected number of youth to be under control is computed by multiplying the base expectancy rate or .03 by the 1972 youth population or 88,316. Additionally, an estimated number of youth to be subject to control is provided which includes the two sibling estimate reported by Family Intervention Staff of the 393 youth directly referred to Diversion's family intervention program.

In summary, the diversion program, similar to boys' center and probation subsidy, influenced the administering of control in two ways. First, the program initiated a displacement process whereby youths formerly viewed as suitable for a previous form of control are judged, within a framework of additional control alternatives, suitable for diversion. This displacement was evidenced by the decrease in 1972 youth arrests, juvenile court intake referrals, and juvenile court petitions, as well as the increase in cases closed at intake or placed under informal probation. This displacement provided some clients for the diversion program. Second, new clients previously not considered for control at all are now judged suitable for diversion. This was demonstrated by the indirect referral of siblings, as well as parents, into diversion's family intervention programs.

Together these findings indicate that diversion's official goal of limiting the jurisdiction of the juvenile court has not been achieved. Instead, diversion has enlarged the scope of the juvenile court and the proportion of population under its control.[24]

[1]Margaret Rosenheim, "Youth Services Bureaus:  A Concept in Search of Definition."  Juvenile Court Judges Journal 20-22 (1969), p. 69.

[2]For a discussion see William H. Sheridan, "Juveniles Who Commit Noncriminal Acts:  Why Treat in a Correction System?"  Federal Probation 31 (1967), pp. 26.

[3]The President's Commission on Law Enforcement and Administration of Justice.  Task Force Report:  Juvenile Delinquency and Youth Crime (1967), p. 8.

[4]President's Task Force Report, p. 8.

[5]President's Task Force Report, p. 8.

[6]President's Task Force Report, p. 8.

[7]President's Task Force Report, p. 9.

[8]President's Task Force Report, p. 9.

[9]U. S. President's Commission on Law Enforcement and Administration of Justice, The Challenge of Crime in a Free Society (1967), p. 83.

[10]President's Task Force Report:  Juvenile Delinquency and Youth Crime, p. 20.

[11]Rosenheim, "Youth Service Bureaus:  A Concept in Search of Definition," p. 70.

[12]For a similar discussion on middle-class families and their access to alternative resources for juvenile problems see Cicourel, The Social Organization of Juvenile Justice, pp. 273-291.

[13]For a discussion of the various Youth Service Bureau program models that have evolved, see Sherwood Norman, "The Youth Service Bureau:  A Brief Description with Five Current Programs," National Council on Crime and Delinquency (New York:  NCCD, 1970), pp. 5-6.

[14]William A. Underwood, "California's Youth Service Bureaus," Youth Authority Quarterly (Winter, 1969), p. 28.

[15]Michael N. Canlis, "Tomorrow is Too Late!" Youth Authority Quarterly (Spring, 1968), p. 10.

[16]California Delinquency Prevention Commission. Youth Service Bureaus, Standards and Guidelines (1968).

[17]Underwood, "California's Youth Service Bureaus," p. 31.

[18]Irving Spergel, Community Problem Solving:  The Delinquency Example (1969), p. 215.

[19]Spergel, Community Problem Solving:  The Delinquency Example, p. 68.

[20]Virginia Satir, Conjoint Family Therapy (1967), p. 44; also see C. Ray Jefferey and Ina A. Jeffery, "Prevention Through the Family," in Amos and Wellford (ed.), Delinquency Prevention Theory and Practice (1967), p. 73.

[21]Edwin Lemert, Instead of Court:  Diversion In Juvenile Justice (DHEW Publication No. (HSM) 72-9093, 1971), p. 71.

[22]This is a simplified version of labeling theory's portrayal of the role of labeling by social control agencies in perpetuating subsequent deviance.  For a more detailed discussion of labeling theory, see T. Scheff, Being Mentally Ill (1966); E. Schur, Labeling Deviant Behavior:  Its Sociological Implications (1971); Becker, "Labeling Theory Reconsidered," in P. Rock and M. McIntosh (eds). Deviance and Social Control (1973), p. 41; Downes and Rock, "Social Reaction to Deviance and Its Effects on Crime and Criminal Careers," Brit. J. Soc. 22 (1971); Erikson, "Notes on the Sociology of Deviance," Social Problems, 9 (1962), p. 307; Warren and Johnson, "A Critique of Labeling Theory from the Phenomenological Perspective," in R. Scott and J. Douglas (eds.), Theoretical Perspectives on Deviance (1972), p. 69; Spitzer, "Labeling and Deviant Behavior:  A Study of Imputation and Reaction in the Definition of Self" (unpublished Ph.D. dissertation, Indiana University, 1971).

[23]To date, efforts to determine if contact with the juvenile justice system increases a youth's delinquent behavior have led to conflicting results at best.  For a comprehensive review of empirical studies related to the effect of juvenile justice labeling, see A. Mahoney, "The Effect of Labeling Upon Youths in the Juvenile Justice System:  A Review of the Evidence," Law and Society Review, 8 (1974), p. 583.  For a more general review of empirical research related to labeling theory's various assumptions, see Wellford, "Labelling Theory and Criminology:  An Assessment,"  Social Problems 22 (1975), p. 332.

[24]For similar elaboration upon diversion's potential to produce accelerated social control see T. Blomberg, "Diversion and Accelerated Social Control," The Journal of Criminal Law and Criminology, 68 (1977), p. 274 and "Diversion from Juvenile Court:  A Review of the Evidence," in F. Faust and P. Brantingham (ed.), Juvenile Justice Philosophy, 2nd Edition (1978).

CHAPTER 6

ACCELERATED SOCIAL CONTROL AND THE FUTURE OF JUVENILE JUSTICE

This study reflects the growing interest in the organization of juvenile court agencies. Although previous juvenile court literature is replete with studies describing the court's humanitarian philosophy and development, little attention has been given to the organization character of the courts. As a result, the literature and empirical findings on juvenile court operations and decision-making have largely been fragmentary and discontinuous.

In approaching the juvenile court as a distinct organization and decision-making system, this study explored a series of court service innovations in terms of the relationship between court organization and decision-making.

To elaborate, the juvenile court has been viewed as a formal organization that operates with conflicting goals, limited technology, and financial instability. These characteristics produce operational uncertainty and result in the juvenile court taking on an adaptable or opportunistic character that facilitates incorporation of varieties of treatment innovations. These innovations, in turn, shape the court's capacity to respond to categories of youth and family problems. Consequently, the type of client handling provided by the court is significantly influenced by the organization context of the juvenile court.[1]

In assessing the background of the boys' center, probation subsidy, and diversion, it has been shown that a concern for financial stability was a major reason the court developed these professional services for youths. Moreover, the court organization was shown to be expansive. If a financial advantage was perceived in maintaining or increasing organization components, the court participated. Thus, the court's expansions related less to the explicit needs of clients than to the court organization's perceived maintenance and growth requirements. The impact of these three court service developments involved both intended client displacements and new client discoveries, which together produced increased control by the court over its youthful clients.

A major question that emerges from these findings is how these various liberal court reforms resulted in increased social control. This question addresses the organizational transformation of reform movements and requires consideration of the character of the juvenile court organization. In considering the organization character of the juvenile court, this study has argued that because the court operates under conditions that produce operational uncertainty, it will respond to program opportunities it perceives as compatible with its organization needs. Moreover, ever-present uncertainty predisposes the court to operationalize reform programs to reinforce previous formal or informal court practices instead of to restructure court operations. Consequently, the court's transformation of these reforms was predictable given the character of the juvenile court organization.

The boys' center, probation subsidy, and diversion developments can be seen as part of a larger movement to alter the nature of juvenile court organization. A major index of this alteration in organization character is the different distribution, over time, in court control meted out to youths and, more recently with diversion, their families. It has been demonstrated that in the last two decades court services have shifted from conducting social history studies and informal and formal home supervision to youths on probation to a correctional establishment complete with diagnostic facilities, intensive home supervision, family intervention services, institution facilities, parole services, and mechanisms for substantial community information-gathering and surveillance. These increases in local court control capacities largely have resulted from conscious state and federal policies that have reduced local autonomy because of increased local dependence on centralized funds and concurrent local submission to centralized authority.

The shift in the local court's organization character has corresponded with the increasing coordination between local, state, and federal correction related agencies. Correctional service expansions at the local level have not led to decreased number or capacity of state correction institutions and related services. Therefore, given this expanding state and local correction network, it appears increasingly likely that a larger proportion of the youth population and families will become subject to some form of state or court control.

Diversion's present role in formalizing family intervention strategies for dealing with problem youths is particularly alarming. Several states either are considering or have already made family intervention compulsory through legislation. Florida, for example, recently enacted legislation authorizing the juvenile court to order parents and guardians of delinquent, dependent, or unruly children to participate in a counseling program deemed necessary for the child's rehabilitation.[2]

Unfortunately, there is no conclusive empirical evidence to indicate that treating the family will be more effective than treating individual youths. As pointed out earlier, studies of the relationship between family characteristics and delinquency have not identified family variables that enable delinquency prediction.[3]

Growing concern over the lack of empirical justification for diversion, family intervention, and related delinquency prevention and control strategies, combined with these approaches' potential to accelerate youth behavior problems, has stimulated research leading to increasing empirical justification for various non-intervention delinquency techniques. Klein, for example, in comparing diversion with other juvenile arrest dispositions, found that fifty-two percent of the youths for whom police requested juvenile court petitions were arrest-free after six months while sixty-seven percent of the youths diverted and referred for service were arrest-free. Moreover, seventy-two percent of the youths who were counseled and released without any form of service were arrest-free after the same time period. Klein concludes that providing diversion services to clients who might otherwise have been released outright may well increase their subsequent delinquency.[4]

A major social policy question for diversion is at what point intervention into the lives of problem youths should occur. Wolfgang, Figlio, and Sellin[5] report in their cohort study of 9,945 boys that forty-six percent of the delinquents were not charged for subsequent delinquent acts after the first offense and that thirty-five percent of the second time offenders were not charged for a third delinquent offense. These findings led the authors to argue that any form of significant treatment intervention before the commission of the third delinquent act would be wasteful. Such findings provide empirical support for "radical non-intervention" strategies, which Schur has summarized as follows:

> In radical nonintervention delinquents are seen not as having special personal characteristics, nor even as being subject to socioeconomic constraints, but rather as suffering from contingencies. Youthful "misconduct," it is argued, is extremely common; delinquents are those youths who, for a variety of reasons, drift into disapproved forms of behavior and are caught and "processed." A great deal of the labeling of delinquents is socially unnecessary and counterproductive. Policies should be adopted, therefore, that accept a greater diversity in youth behavior; special delinquency laws should be exceedingly narrow in scope or else abolished completely, along with preventive efforts that single out specific individuals and programs that employ "compulsory treatment." For those serious offenses that cannot simply be defined away through a greater tolerance of diversity, this reaction pattern may paradoxically increase "criminalization"--uniformly applied punishment not disguised as treatment; increased formalization of whatever juvenile court procedures remain, in order to limit sanctioning to cases where actual antisocial acts have been committed and to provide constitutional safeguards for those proceeded against.[6]

Nonetheless, and despite growing recognition and interest in non-intervention delinquency approaches, expanding diversion and related community-based delinquency prevention and control methods appears to be the trend in future administration of juvenile justice and youth corrections. Accelerated social control now and in the future of juvenile justice appears to be not only the rhetoric of social policy critics but also the reality of the era.

[1]For further specification of the relationship between the juvenile court's organization characteristics and decision-making see T. Blomberg, "The Juvenile Court As An Organization and Decision-Making System," International Journal of Comparative and Applied Criminal Justice, 1 (1977) p. 135.

[2]Section 39.11(7), Florida Statutes (1975).

[3]For discussion see, e.g., Travis Hirschi and Hanan Selvin, "False Criteria of Causality," in M. Wolfgang, L. Savitz and N. Johnston (eds.) The Sociology of Crime and Delinquency (1966); Causes of Delinquency (1969); Jeffery, C. Ray and Ina Jeffery, "Prevention Through the Family," in W. Amos and C. Wellford (eds.) Delinquency Prevention: Theory and Practice (1967), p. 73. Karen Wilkinson, "The Broken Family and Juvenile Delinquency: Scientific Explanation or Ideology," Social Problems, 21 (1974).

[4]M. Klein, Alternative Dispositions for Juvenile Offenders (1975) and Pivotal Ingredients of Police Juvenile Diversion Programs (1975).

[5]M. Wolfgang, R. Figlio, and T. Sellin, Delinquency in a Birth Cohort (1972), p. 25.

[6]Edwin Schur, Radical Non-Intervention: Rethinking the Delinquency Problem (1973), p. 23.

BIBLIOGRAPHY

Adams, Richard N. and Jack J. Preiss (eds.), Human Organization
Research: Field Relations and Techniques. Homewood,
Illinois: Dorsey Press, Inc., 1960.

American Friends Service Committee, Struggle for Justice. New
York: Hill and Wang, Inc., 1971.

Banfield, Edward C. and James Q. Wilson. City Politics. New
York: Random House, Inc., 1963.

Baron, Roger and Floyd Feeney. Preventing Delinquency Through
Diversion - The Sacramento County Probation Department 601
Diversion Project: A First Year Report. Center on Adminis-
tration of Criminal Justice, University of California,
Davis, May, 1972.

Blau, Peter M. The Dynamics of Bureaucracy: A Study of Inter-
personal Relations in Two Government Agencies. Chicago:
University of Chicago Press, 1963, pp. 269-301.

Blau, Peter M. and Richard Scott. Formal Organizations: A Comparative Approach. San Francisco: Chandler Publishing
Company, 1962.

Blumberg, Abraham S. Criminal Justice. Chicago: Quadrangle
Books, 1967.

Briar, Scott and Irving Piliavin, "Police Encounters with Juveniles," in Rose Giallombardo (ed.), Juvenile Delinquency: A
Book of Readings. New York: John Wiley and Sons, Inc.,
1966.

Cahn, Frances and Valeska Bary. Welfare Activities of Federal,
State and Local Governments in California 1850-1934. Berkeley: University of California Press, 1936, pp. 46-102.

Carter, Robert M. and Leslie T. Wilkins (eds.), Probation and
Parole: Selected Readings. New York: John Wiley and Sons,
Inc., 1970.

Cicourel, Aaron. Measurement in Sociology. New York: The Free
Press, 1964, pp. 14-25.

Cicourel, Aaron. The Social Organization of Juvenile Justice.
New York: John Wiley and Sons, Inc., 1968.

Cicourel, Aaron V. and John I. Kitsuse. The Educational Decision-
Makers. New York: The Bobbs-Merrill Company, Inc., 1963,
pp. 3-33.

Clark, Burton.  Adult Education in Transition:  A Study of Insti-
     tutional Insecurity.  Berkeley-Los Angeles:  University of
     California Press, 1958.

Clark, Burton.  The Open Door College:  A Case Study.  New York:
     McGraw-Hill Book Co., 1960.

Cohn, Alvin W.  Decision - Making in the Administration of Proba-
     tion Services:  A Descriptive Study of the Probation Manager.
     (unpublished doctoral dissertation), University of Califor-
     nia, Berkeley, 1972.

Cole, George F.  Criminal Justice:  Law and Politics.  North
     Scituate, Massachusetts and Belmont, California:  Duxbury
     Press, 1972.

Cole, George F.  Politics and the Administration of Justice.
     Beverly Hills:  Sage Publications, Inc., 1973.

Cressey, Donald R., "Achievement of an Unstated Organizational
     Goal:  An Observation on Prisons," Pacific Sociological
     Review 1 (1958), pp. 43-49.

Davis, George, "A Study of Adult Probation Violation Rates by
     Means of the Cohort Approach," The Journal of Criminal Law
     and Criminology and Police Science.  (March, 1964).

Deutsch, Albert.  Our Rejected Children.  Boston:  Little, Brown
     and Company, 1947.

Dressler, David.  Practice and Theory of Probation and Parole.
     New York and London:  Columbia University Press, 1959.

Emerson, Robert M.  Judging Delinquents Context and Process in
     Juvenile Court.  Chicago:  Aldine Publishing Co., 1969.

Etzioni, Amitai.  Modern Organizations.  Englewood Cliffs, New
     Jersey:  Prentice-Hall, Inc., 1964.

Freeman, Howard E. and Clarence C. Sherwood.  Social Research and
     Social Policy.  Englewood Cliffs, New Jersey:  Prentice
     Hall, Inc., 1970.

Galbraith, John Kenneth.  Economics and the Public Purpose.
     Boston:  Houghton Mifflin Company, 1973, pp. 81-169.

Galbraith, John Kenneth, The New Industrial State.  New York:
     The New American Library, Inc., 1968 (originally published
     Boston:  Houghton Mifflin Company, 1967).

Goldman, Nathan.  The Differential Selection of Juvenile Offenders
     for Court Appearance.  Washington, D. C.:  National Council
     on Crime and Delinquency, 1963.

Gore, William J.  Administrative Decision-Making:  A Heuristic

Model. New York: John Wiley and Sons, Inc., 1964.

Gusfield, Joseph. Symbolic Crusade: Status Politics and the American Temperance Movement. Urbana: University of Illinois Press, 1963.

Harlow, Eleanor, "Diversion from the Criminal Justice System," National Council on Crime and Delinquency, Crime and Delinquency Literature. 2 (April 1970), pp. 136-164.

Jeffery, C. Ray. Crime Prevention Through Environmental Design. Beverly Hills and London: Sage Publications, 1971, pp. 167-174.

Jeffery, C. Ray and Ina A. Jeffery, "Prevention Through the Family," in William E. Amos and Charles F. Wellford (eds.), Delinquency Prevention Theory and Practice. New York: Prentice-Hall, Inc., 1967, pp. 73-98.

Kassebaum, Gene, "Strategies for the Sociological Study of Criminal Corectional Systems," in Robert W. Habenstein (ed.), Pathways to Data: Field Methods for Studying Ongoing Social Organizations. Chicago: Aldine Publishing Company, 1970, pp. 122-138.

Lemert, Edwin. Social Action and Legal Change. Chicago: Aldine Press, 1970.

Levine, Sol and Paul E. White, "Exchange as a Conceptual Framework for the Study of Interorganizational Relationships," in Amitai Etzioni (ed.), A Sociological Reader on Complex Organizations, Second Edition. New York: Holt, Rinehart and Winston, Inc., 1969, pp. 117-132.

Litterer, Joseph A. Organizations: Structure and Behavior. New York: John Wiley and Sons, Inc., 1963, pp. 276-344.

Lofland, John. Analyzing Social Settings. Belmont, California: Wadsworth Publishing Company, Inc., 1971.

MacIver, Robert M. The Prevention and Control of Delinquency. New York: Atherton Press, 1966.

March, James G. and Herbert A. Simon. Organizations. New York: John Wiley and Sons, Inc., 1958.

Matza, David. Becoming Deviant. Englewood Cliffs, New Jersey: Prentice-Hall, Inc., 1969.

Matza, David. Delinquency and Drift. New York: John Wiley and Sons, Inc., 1964.

Messinger, Sheldon L., "Organizational Transformation: A Case Study of Declining Social Movement," American Sociological Review, 20 (1955), pp. 3-10.

Messinger, Sheldon L., "Strategies of Control," (unpublished doctoral dissertation), University of California, Los Angeles, 1969, pp. 138-190, 237-299.

Michels, Robert. Political Parties: A Sociological Study of the Oligarchical Tendencies of Modern Democracy. New York: The Free Press, 1962.

Miller, Frank W., et al. The Juvenile Justice Process. Mineola, New York: Foundation Press, Inc., 1971.

Mouzelis, Nicos P. Organisation and Bureaucracy: An Analysis of Modern Theories. Chicago: Aldine Publishing Company, 1967, pp. 120-177.

Nonet, Philippe. Administrative Justice: Advocacy and Change in Government Agencies. New York: Russell Sage Foundation, 1969.

Norman, Sherwood. The Youth Service Bureau: A Brief Description with Five Current Programs. New York: National Council on Crime and Delinquency, June, 1970.

Olsen, Marvin E. The Process of Social Organization. New York: Holt, Rinehart and Winston, Inc., 1968, pp. 211-348.

Packer, Herbert L., "Two Models of the Criminal Process," University of Pennsylvania Law Review, 113 (1964), pp. 1-68.

Perlman, Robert and Arnold Gurin. Community Organization and Social Planning. New York: John Wiley and Sons, Inc., 1972, pp. 33-152.

Perrow, Charles. Complex Organizations: A Critical Essay. Glenview, Illinois: Scott, Foresman and Company, 1972, pp. 177-204.

Perrow, Charles. Organizational Analysis: A Sociological View. Belmont, California: Brooks/Cole Publishing Company, 1970.

Piliavan, Irving and Carl Werthman, "Gang Members and the Police," in David Bordua (ed.), The Police: Six Sociological Essays. New York: John Wiley and Sons, Inc., 1967.

Platt, Anthony M. The Child Savers. Chicago and London: The University of Chicago Press, 1969.

Platt, Anthony M., "The Triumph of Benevolence: The Origins of the Juvenile Justice System in the United States," in Abraham Blumberg (ed.), Introduction to Criminology. New York: Random House, 1972.

Rosenheim, Margaret. Justice for the Child: A Juvenile Court in Transition. New York: The Free Press of Glencoe, 1962, pp. 82-235.

Rosenheim, Margaret, "Youth Service Bureaus:  A Concept in Search of Definition," Juvenile Court Judges Journal, 20 (Summer, 1969), pp. 69-74.

Rothman, David J.  The Discovery of the Asylum.  Boston and Toronto:  Little, Brown and Company, 1971, pp. 79-108, 206-236.

Satir, Virginia.  Conjoint Family Therapy.  Palo Alto:  Science and Behavior Books, Inc., 1967.

Scott, W. Richard, "Field Methods in the Study of Organization," in James G. March (ed.), Handbook of Organizations.  Chicago:  Rand McNally and Company, 1965, pp. 261-304.

Selznick, Philip, "Foundations of a Theory of Organization," American Sociological Review.  13 (1948), pp. 25-35.

Selznick, Philip.  Law, Society and Industrial Justice.  New York:  Russell Sage Foundation, 1969, pp. 11-18.

Selznick, Philip.  Leadership in Administration.  Evanston, Illinois:  Row Peterson, 1957.

Selznick, Philip.  TVA and the Grass Roots.  New York:  Harper Row, Inc., 1966 (originally published Berkeley and Los Angeles:  University of California Press, 1949), pp. 249-266.

Sheridan, William H., "Juveniles Who Commit Noncriminal Acts: Why Treat in a Correction System?"  Federal Probation.  31 (1967), pp. 26-36.

Simon, Herbert A.  Administrative Behavior:  A Study of Decision-Making Processes in Administrative Organization.  New York:  The Free Press, 1965, pp. 1-79.

Skolnick, Jerome H.  Justice Without Trial:  Law Enforcement in Democratic Society.  New York:  John Wiley and Sons, Inc., 1966.

Smith, Robert L., "Youth and Correction:  An Institutional Analysis of the California Youth Authority," (unpublished master's thesis), University of California, Berkeley, 1955.

Spergel, Irving A.  Community Organization:  Studies in Constraint.  Beverly Hills and London:  Sage Publications, 1972.

Spergel, Irving A.  Community Problem:  Solving the Delinquency Example.  Chicago:  The University of Chicago Press, 1969.

Street, David, Robert Vinter and Charles Perrow.  Organizations for Treatment.  New York:  The Free Press, 1966.

Sudnow, David, "The Public Defender," in Richard D. Swartz and

Jerome H. Skolnick (eds.), Society and the Legal Order. New York: Basic Books, Inc., 1970.

Sykes, Gresham M. The Society of Captives: A Study of a Maximum Security Prison. Princeton: Princeton University Press, 1958.

Thompson, James D. and William J. McEwen, "Organizational Goals and Environment," in Amitai Etzioni (ed.), A Sociological Reader on Complex Organizations, Second Edition. New York: Holt, Rinehart and Winston, Inc., 1969, pp. 187-196.

Transactions of the Commonwealth Club of California, Vol. V. San Francisco, 1910.

Walton, Clarence C. Corporate Social Responsibilities. Belmont, California: Wadsworth Publishing Company, Inc., 1967.

Ward, Richard H., "The Labeling Theory: A Critical Analysis," Criminology: An Interdisciplinary Journal. 9 (August - November 1971), pp. 268-290.

Warren, Marguerite, "The Case for Differential Treatment of Delinquents," in Harwin L. Voss (ed.), Society, Delinquency and Delinquent Behavior. Boston: Little, Brown and Company, 1970, pp. 419-430.

Wheeler, Stanton (ed.), Controlling Delinquents. New York: John Wiley and Sons, Inc., 1968, pp. 31-102.

Wilkins, Leslie T. Evaluation of Penal Measures. New York: Random House, Inc., 1969.

Wolin, Sheldon S., "A Critique of Organizational Theories," in Amitai Etzioni (ed.), A Sociological Reader on Complex Organizations. Second Edition. New York: Holt, Rinehart and Winston, Inc., 1969, pp. 133-149.

Zald, Mayer N., "The Correctional Institution for Juvenile Offenders: An Analysis of Organizational 'Character,'" Social Problems. 8 (Summer, 1960), pp. 57-67.


County Documents and Publications

Juvenile Justice Commission. Annual Report. County Probation Department, yearly reports from 1957-1972.

Annual Report of the Probation Officer, County Probation Administration, yearly reports from 1940-1972.

Monthly Comparative Statistics. County Probation Administration, monthly reports January, 1957 through December, 1972.

State Documents and Publications

Board of Corrections. Correction in the Community: Alternatives
to Incarceration. Sacramento: State of California, June,
1964.

Board of Corrections. Field Services: Correctional System Study.
Sacramento: State of California, July, 1971.

Board of Corrections. Institutions: Correctional System Study.
Sacramento: State of California, July, 1971.

Board of Corrections. The System: Correctional System Study.
Sacramento: State of California, July, 1971.

Bureau of Criminal Statistics. Adult and Juvenile Probation 1972.
Sacramento: State of California, Department of Justice,
1973.

Bureau of Criminal Statistics. Delinquency and Probation in California. Sacramento: State of California, Department of
Justice, yearly reports from 1957-1964.

Bureau of Criminal Statistics. Juvenile Probation. Sacramento:
State of California, Department of Justice, yearly reports
from 1969-1971.

Bureau of Criminal Statistics. Juvenile Probation Extended Data.
Sacramento: State of California, Department of Justice,
yearly reports from 1965-1968.

California Council on Criminal Justice. Annual Report 1971.
Sacramento: State of California, January, 1972, pp. 1-7.

California Delinquency Prevention Commission. Youth Service
Bureaus, Standards and Guidelines. Sacramento: State of
California, October, 1968.

California Youth Authority. Delinquency Causes and Remedies:
The Working Assumptions of California Youth Authority Staff.
Sacramento: State of California, February, 1972.

California Youth Authority. Program Planning Policy. Sacramento:
State of California, April, 1971.

California Youth Authority. Youth Service Bureaus in California,
Progress Report Number 3. Sacramento; State of California,
January, 1972.

Canlis, Michael N., "Tomorrow is Too Late," Youth Authority
Quarterly. 21 (Spring, 1968), pp. 9-16.

Department of the Youth Authority. California Laws Relating to
Youthful Offenders: The Youth Authority Act and The Juvenile Court Law. (California Welfare and Institutions Code).

Sacramento: State of California, January, 1968.

Department of the Youth Authority. Probation Subsidy Programs. Sacramento: State of California, May, 1973.

Department of the Youth Authority. Youth Service Bureaus: A National Study. Washington, D. C., U. S. Government Printing Office, Department of Health, Education and Welfare, November, 1972.

Duxbury, Elaine, "Youth Service Bureaus - California Style," Youth Authority Quarterly. 24 (Summer, 1971), pp. 11-17.

Governor's Select Committee on Law Enforcement Problems. Controlling Crime in California. Sacramento: State of California, August, 1973, pp. 67-76.

Governor's Special Study Commission on Juvenile Justice. Report. Sacramento: State of California, 1960.

Pezman, T. L., "Untwisting the Twisted," Probation Camps in California. Sacramento: State of California, Camps, Ranches and Schools Division, July, 1963.

Preston School of Industry. Fourth Biennial Report of the Board of Trustees 1898-1900, Preston. Sacramento: State of California, 1900.

Underwood, William A. "California's Youth Service Bureaus," Youth Authority Quarterly. (Winter, 1969), pp. 27-33.

Vaughn, Roley, "A Century of County Camps," California Youth Authority. 17 (Fall, 1964), pp. 26-31.


Federal Documents and Publications

Lemert, Edwin. Instead of Court: Diversion in Juvenile Justice. Washington, D. C.: U. S. Government Printing Office, Department of Health, Education and Welfare, 1971.

Rubin, Ted. Law as an Agent of Delinquency Prevention. Washington, D. C.: U. S. Government Printing Office, Department of Health, Education and Welfare, 1971.

Smith, Robert L. A Quiet Revolution: Probation Subsidy. Washington, D. C.: U. S. Government Printing Office, Department of Health, Education and Welfare, 1971.

Turk, Austin T. Legal Sanctioning and Social Control. Washington, D. C.: U. S. Government Printing Office, Department of Health, Education and Welfare, 1972.

U. S. President's Commission on Law Enforcement and Administra-

tion of Justice. <u>The Challenge of Crime in a Free Society</u>.
    Washington, D. C.:  U. S. Government Printing Office, 1967,
    pp. 55-89, 279-291.

U. S. President's Commission on Law Enforcement and Administra-
    tion of Justice. <u>Task Force Report:  Juvenile Delinquency</u>
    <u>and Youth Crime</u>. Washington, D. C.:  U. S. Government
    Printing Office, 1967.

Warren, Marguerite. <u>Correctional Treatment in Community Settings:</u>
    <u>A Report of Current Research</u>. Washington, D. C.:  U. S.
    Government Printing Office, Department of Health, Education
    and Welfare, 1972.

Youth Development and Delinquency Prevention Administration.  <u>The</u>
    <u>Challenge of Youth Service Bureaus</u>. Washington, D. C.:
    U. S. Government Printing Office, Department of Health,
    Education and Welfare, 1973.


Becker, Howard. "Labeling Theory Reconsider," in P. Rock and M.
    McIntosh (eds.), <u>Deviance and Social Control</u> 41, 1973.

Blomberg, Thomas. "Diversion and Accelerated Social Control,"
    <u>The Journal of Criminal Law and Criminology</u> 68, No. 2
    (1977), pp. 274-282.

Blomberg, Thomas. "Diversion from Juvenile Court:  A Review of
    the Evidence," in F. Faust and P. Brantingham (ed.), <u>Juven-</u>
    <u>ile Justice Philosophy</u>, 2nd Edition. Minneapolis, Minn.:
    West Publishing Co., 1978.

Blomberg, Thomas. "The Juvenile Court As An Organization and
    Decision-Making System," <u>International Journal of Compara-</u>
    <u>tive and Applied Criminal Justice</u> 1, No. 2 (1977), pp. 135-
    145.

Downs, David and Paul Rock. "Social Reaction to Deviance and Its
    Effects on Crime and Criminal Careers," <u>British Journal of</u>
    <u>Sociology</u> 22 (1971), p. 351.

Erikson, Kai. "Notes on the Sociology of Deviance," <u>Social Prob-</u>
    <u>lems</u> 9 (1962), p. 307.

Hirschi, Travis. Causes of Delinquency. Berkeley:  University
    of California Press, 1969.

Hirschi, Travis and Hanan Selvin, "False Criteria of Causality,"
    in M. Wolfgang, L. Savitz, and N. Johnston (eds.), <u>The</u>
    <u>Sociology of Crime and Delinquency</u>. New York:  John Wiley
    and Sons, Inc., 1966.

Klein, Malcolm. <u>Alternative Dispositions for Juvenile Offenders</u>.
    Los Angeles, California:  University of Southern California,
    1975.

Klein, Malcolm. Pivotal Ingredients of Police Juvenile Diversion. Los Angeles, California: University of Southern California, 1975.

Mahoney, Anne Rankin. "The Effect of Labeling Upon Youths in the Juvenile Justice System: A Review of the Evidence," Law and Society Review 8 (1974), p. 583-609.

Scheff, Thomas. Being Mentally Ill. Chicago: Aldine, 1966.

Schur, Edwin. Labeling Deviant Behavior: Its Sociological Implications. New York: Harper and Row, 1971

Schur, Edwin. Radical Non-Intervention: Rethinking the Delinquency Problem. Englewood Cliffs, New Jersey: Prentice-Hall, Inc., 1973.

Spitzer, Steven. "Labeling and Deviant Behavior: A Study of Imputation and Reaction in the Definition of Self. Unpublished Ph.D. dissertation, Indiana University, 1971.

Warren, Carol and John Johnson. "A Critique of Labeling Theory from the Phenomenological Perspective," in Robert Scott and Jack Douglas (eds.) Theoretical Perspectives on Deviance. New York: Basic Books, 1972.

Wellford, Charles. "Labelling Theory and Criminology: An Assessment," Social Problems 22 (1975), pp. 332-345.

Wilkinson, Karen. "The Broken Family and Juvenile Delinquency: Scientific Explanation or Ideology," Social Problems 21 (1974), pp. 726-739.

Wolfgang, Marvin, Robert Figlio and Thorsten Sellin. Delinquency in Birth Cohort. Chicago: University of Chicago Press, 1972.

California Youth Authority and Adult Corrections Agenct. Report (1967), pp. 89-90.

Section 39.11(7), Florida Statutes (1975).

# APPENDIX

## DESCRIPTION OF RESEARCH METHODS

This study's methodological approach was that of field work. Overall, field work research emphasizes the perspective of the actors (i.e.: organization personnel) as a significant variable in the understanding of organization action. The essential concern for an organization field worker is in the discovery and description of the ongoing social organization produced by organization personnel. Schutz summarizes:

> The observational field of the social scientist . . . has a specific meaning and relevance structure for the human beings living, acting and thinking therein. By a series of common-sense constructs they have preselected and pre-interpreted this world which they experience as the reality of their daily lives. It is these thought objects of theirs which determine their behavior by motivating it. The thought objects constructed by the social scientist, in order to grasp the social reality, have to be founded upon the thought objects constructed by the common-sense thinking of men, living their daily lives within their social world.[1]

Research for this study progressed for three years. Previously, the researcher spent two years as a part-time employee of this county's probation department. The initial research procedure involved an immersion into the juvenile court and probation department to the extent possible for a nonparticipant. The basic method used for gathering information and data included observations, interviewing, and document analysis.

Most observations were conducted at various interdepartmental meetings, budgetary planning meetings, and probation administrative meetings between the county probation officer and the county auditor, Board of Supervisor's representatives, and immediate administrative and supervisory staff. In addition, the researcher attended several California Youth Authority and California Council on Criminal Justice regional meetings. The attempt was to gain an understanding of the county juvenile court and probation department in action both internally and with its significant environment.

Informal interviewing provided the primary techniques for gaining information on administrative problems, thinking, and action. In the beginning, a substantial amount of time was spent interviewing individuals with various ties to the county's juvenile court and probation department (i.e.: juvenile court judges, probation personnel, local and state officials, and representatives of community organizations). The basic concern was in determining the kinds of internal and external problems, pressures, opportunities, and exchange relationships involved in moving the local court system toward change or development.

The interview mechanics involved covering specific subjects and questions in each session. However, the conversations were allowed to drift according to the particular area of familiarity or expertise of the respondent, rather than having him answer a fixed set of questions. This flexible interview procedure was particularly useful in the exploratory stages of this research. The researcher was able to arrive at the problems and thinking of the respondents instead of having them deal with issues that might have seemed relevant. The informal interviewing data were controlled by cross-checking responses whenever possible with recorded or published materials.

In this study, documentary and statistical analysis has provided specific data regarding both major organization decisions and their overall system impact. Generally, problems, decisions, and policy determinations are recorded in some form. In addition, particular court and probation statistics reflect organization activity related to client-handling. However, the gathering of direct proof is limited in organizations. Instead, reliance is on a number of indirect or partial indicators that together can provide an accurate interpretation. Burton Clark provides a relevant appraisal of the formal methodological weakness of this form of organization research.

He states:

> An institutional study involves a search for the significant factors in a complex situation of social action. A strong point in such studies is their relevance to real problems and to significant aspects of behavior in a given situation. The orientations fruitful in such a search, however, naturally favor an emphasis upon discovery and less emphasis on close, immediate validation of research results. Moreover, the use of formal techniques is limited if the inquiry takes place within organizations, and the possibilities of clear and direct proof are thereby narrowed . . . The lack of immediate validation is defensible in that the ultimate validity of all research rests not in the tests of significance of the moment, but upon whether the findings hang together with findings from other studies to produce a theoretical structure.[2]

FOOTNOTES--APPENDIX

[1]Alfred Schutz, "Concept and Theory Formation in the Social Sciences," The Journal of Philosophy 51 (April, 1954), pp. 266-267.

[2]Burton Clark, Adult Education in Transition:  A Study of Institutional Insecurity (Berkeley - Los Angeles:  University of California Press, 1958), p. 167.